THE
TEST
DESIGN
HANDBOOK

THE TEST DESIGN HANDBOOK

CAROL COPPERUD

Educational Technology Publications
Englewood Cliffs, New Jersey   07632

Library of Congress Cataloging in Publication Data

Copperud, Carol.
   The test design handbook.

   Bibliography: p.
   Includes index.
   1. Educational tests and measurements—Handbooks,
manuals, etc. I. Title.
LB1131.C5478   371.2'61   79-361
ISBN 0-87778-136-2

Printed in the United States of America.

Library of Congress Catalog Card Number:
79-361.

International Standard Book Number:
0-87778-136-2.

First Printing: July, 1979.

Acknowledgments

This book grew out of an HEW project in which I participated at the University of California, San Francisco. I assisted nursing faculty in the western United States in the development of methods and tools for assessing their students' performance in the classroom as well as clinical settings. With the encouragement of these nurses, I pursued the idea of writing this book to address the similar testing problems encountered by teachers of any subject, at any level, in any setting.

My greatest help came from my associates at UCSF who discussed my ideas with me, contributed worthy suggestions to the content, and critiqued the drafts. I am grateful for their continued input, support, and encouragement.

My family was also a constant source of not only moral support, but also professional support. My thanks to my aunt and uncle for the peace and quiet of their study, and to my mother, who implemented these ideas in her own teaching and spread the good word about testing to her colleagues.

Finally, my special thanks go to Brian Ogle, whose timely birth gave his mother, Barbara, time off from her job so she could stay home and type, proofread, and critique this document. It was a long, hard job, well done.

Preface

Instructors are being looked on more and more as the culprits in an educational system which does not seem to be as adequate as it once was. Parents, taxpayers, students, and legislators are all demanding that we as teachers be held accountable for our students' learning.

This book does not intend to address or investigate the complexities of our modern-day educational system. It is designed, however, to help you as a teacher respond to the critics. Even if your teaching is not being challenged, it is the objective of this book to give you some basic skills in finding out precisely what your students have learned. This book will help you to design good tests which you can rely on with confidence to measure the effectiveness of your instruction.

Of course, many books have been written on the subject of designing classroom tests. Most graduate programs in education include at least one class in tests and measurement. Unfortunately, for overworked classroom teachers and for the ever-increasing group of instructors in business and industry, this wealth of sophisticated information is often beyond reach. The books run at least 400 pages in length, the courses are costly, and they require background in statistics. Somehow, over the years the gap between the researchers in education and the classroom instructor actually doing the teaching has not been bridged in the area of testing; in fact, the gap seems to be widening, as the researchers become ever more sophisticated and learned.

This book is a condensation of those hefty volumes and classes. While the statistics and technical language have been discarded, the content of this handbook is consistent with their theories. This book is designed to bring the basics of the research into the classroom. If you decide you want to delve more deeply into the topic of tests and measurements, you might start by consulting the books listed in the Bibliography. This book, however, is not meant to be studied as much as it is meant to be *used*. Refer to it every time you write a test.

The primary emphasis of this book is on actually constructing tests. The first six chapters are devoted to the paper-pencil tests you design for testing intellectual or cognitive learning. Learning objectives form the cornerstone of any test, whether it be an essay, multiple-choice, true-false, or short answer test. These six chapters show how to make your tests reflect your instructional objectives. They also give suggestions for improving the technical design of the various types of questions you can include in a paper-pencil test.

Chapters 7 and 8 discuss ways of evaluating students' performances, skills, attitudes, values, and the products they make. Methods of observing your students are presented as well as suggestions for designing the tools used to record these observations, namely, the checklist, rating scale, and anecdotal notes.

Finally, Chapter 9 describes how to assemble the components of effective testing into a complete system.

Tests do not exist, however, in a vacuum. In order to fulfill their function of providing you with accurate information about the extent of a student's learning, tests must be planned and administered systematically. The second objective of this book is to present some methods for making testing an efficient and useful part of instruction. The premise is that testing is as much an integral part of instruction as are the learning activities. Unfortunately, tests take time, energy, and expertise to write. The suggestions in this book are intended to minimize these constraints. By incorporating these suggestions, you will find that your tests will serve as increasingly valuable sources of information about the success of your instruction.

The guidelines in this book are based on some underlying assumptions. One of these assumptions is that you have formulated some ideas concerning what your students are to learn, and that these expectations are valid and reasonable. A corollary to this assumption is that you will indeed structure the classroom learning activities around these expectations. That is, it is assumed that you actually will teach your students the behaviors you said they would learn. This assumption should go without saying, but it is of great importance. Your instructional activities are the link between your original objectives and the tests. If your test is based on the objectives, but your instruction isn't, you cannot hope to have a meaningful test.

A second assumption of this book is that you *want* to use tests as a tool for finding out what your students have learned. In other words, you do not see tests as (a) just an unavoidable task in the instructional process, or (b) as a means of punishing or otherwise intimidating students. The overwhelming bias of this book is that students and teachers are allies in the instructional/testing process. The information derived from tests can help both you and your students in the teaching and learning process. It follows, then, that every test should be as fair as possible—so that students have every chance to demonstrate what they have learned.

This book does not discuss the issue of grading. Even though grades are the usual conclusion of a testing program, they are usually determined in accordance with an established school policy. For example, there are letter grades, number grades, inflated grades, Pass-No Pass, Pass-No Credit, conditional Pass, bell-shaped curves—the list is endless. Since so many local factors are involved in assigning a grade, this book will not be concerned with the topic.

Essentially, then, this handbook is a practical guide to help you gain the most information about your students' learning in the most reliable, efficient ways possible.

C. C.

Table of Contents

THE
TEST
DESIGN
HANDBOOK

Chapter 1

Knowing the Language of Testing

The guidelines for writing tests which are described in this book are based on a few basic principles. It will be useful for you to know what some of these principles are and to know the language associated with them.

The words *test item* will be used interchangeably with the words *test question*. Items or questions are the pieces of the *test* or *exam*. This book will give you suggestions for improving both your individual test questions and the test as a whole.

Tests are one method for giving students an opportunity to show you what they know or what they can do—hopefully, as the result of your instruction. One normally assumes that the scores obtained from these tests are a mirror of the students' true knowledge and abilities. For a test score to be an accurate reflection, however, you must design an instrument which does not distort or obscure the image. This fact becomes even more important if you wish to make decisions about a student's future or statements about his* worth or

---

*A note about the he, he/she, (s)he, he and/or she debate. While this author recognizes that students come in both varieties, for simplicity's sake (one of the goals of this book), the archaic form "he" will be used to designate students of either gender.

capabilities. A fun-house mirror can provoke a lot of laughs, but no one wants to have its reflection presented to the world as a true image.

When designing tests which will provide an accurate reflection, we are concerned primarily with two characteristics. These are known as the test's *validity* and its *reliability*.

A valid test is one which measures what it is intended to measure. Using the mirror analogy, we have chosen a valid tool if we are interested in "measuring" or viewing a person's physical appearance. However, it is not a valid tool if we use it to view a person's skeletal system. More to the point, if you have an interest in knowing what your students have learned about the Stock Exchange in your course in economics, you would not give them a test which asks them questions about personal income tax laws. Similarly, if you want to see if your students can merely recall the steps in a procedure, your test will not include questions which ask them to provide historical justification for the procedure or to defend the order of the steps in the procedure.

The suggestions in this book are presented so that you can be sure your tests are valid. A general rule for ensuring that your tests are valid is to be very clear about what you are trying to find out about a student, and then to be very sure your questions give the student the best opportunity to demonstrate what you are trying to find out—no more, no less.

In addition to validity, the other aspect of a test that we will be concerned with is its reliability. A reliable test is one that you can count on to give consistent results. You would not trust the reading of a bathroom scale which fluctuates according to humidity or has a loose spring. If someone is looking at your students' test scores, they want to be sure these scores are not the result of chance factors or due to variations in directions, scoring, or testing conditions.

There are many factors which affect the reliability of a

test. The suggestions presented in this book specifically address these factors. These suggestions represent three main factors which can affect reliability:

1. *The question itself.* Poorly worded, confusing, ambiguous questions will not yield reliable measures of a student's learning.

2. *Test administration.* Environmental factors, such as heat, lighting, noise, differences in test directions, amount of testing time allowed to different students, confusing instructions, or illegible test sheets can all affect a student's score. The more these factors interfere with a student's attempts to demonstrate what he has learned, the less you can trust his test scores.

3. *Scoring.* Subjective scoring—or scoring which reflects the grader's personal opinions—is more unreliable than objective scoring. In subjectively scored tests, such as essay tests, variations in scores may occur as a result of the grader's fatigue, mental outlook, personal biases, or level of concentration. In other words, a student's score may not necessarily represent his true learning. In objectively scored tests, such as multiple-choice tests, there is no element of grader subjectivity, and therefore the test results are more reliable.

Chapter Summary

All the suggestions and guidelines in this book are offered so that your tests will be more valid and reliable than they may be right now.

Validity and reliability are not important in and of themselves. Rather, their presence insures that you can be sure your students have learned what the test scores indicate they have learned. Most of us need more than intuitive evidence

that we have written good tests. Designing your tests around
the general principles of validity and reliability will increase
your confidence in the meaningfulness of your students' test
scores.

Chapter 2

Relating Test Content
to Course Content

"You never taught us that!" How many times have teachers heard this student complaint during a test? Sometimes, perhaps, they may even be right! The focus of this chapter is on creating a test which *tests* only what you intend to *teach*.

The first step in designing a test is to have a clear idea of what you are trying to measure or find out. For example, you may want to know if your students have learned to multiply fractions accurately, or if they have memorized the Gettysburg Address. Some teachers just want to know if their students have read the assigned chapter. In order to measure something, that "something" must lend itself to being measured. This leads us to that "favorite activity" of teachers —writing learning objectives.

Consider the teacher who uses an assigned text for one semester of English. He periodically gives tests to see if the students have "learned the Unit." At the end of a semester, he turns in grades based on interesting mathematical averages and bell-shaped curves. Ask this same teacher (or the students themselves) what they can now do as a result of this instruction, and you may get one of the following responses: no response at all, or some statement about how they "learned about" some early American novelists such as Hawthorne or Melville. There is no clear picture about what these students can do as a result of their interaction with an assigned text on American literature. Unfortunately, as many parents and embarrassed school officials are finding out, many of these students can actually *do* very little indeed.

This hypothetical English teacher represents a hopefully vanishing breed. Teachers are realizing more and more the necessity for writing objectives. Learning objectives, or behavioral objectives, serve a dual purpose. First of all, they act as an outline for instruction. They help both teachers and students focus on the expectations of the course. Secondly, and more importantly for our purposes, objectives form the basis for testing the student to see what he has learned. Objectives form the reference point against which a student's behavior can be compared. The test provides the student with a structured opportunity to demonstrate this comparison.

In order to use objectives as a reference point, they must be stated in clear, understandable terms. Objectives must provide a statement of observable, expected behaviors—otherwise, what will you compare future behavior to?

The classic formula for writing objectives comes from Robert Mager. According to him, a complete objective has three elements:

(1) an action or behavior that the student is to perform;
(2) the conditions under which these actions are to be performed; and
(3) the criteria or standards for saying whether these actions have been performed satisfactorily.

The most important of these three elements is the behavior. For shorthand purposes, a statement of only the expected behavior often serves as the complete objective. The best way to write an objective which includes behavioral terms is to use action verbs. The list of verbs is endless but includes the following:

identify	distinguish
describe	construct
demonstrate	predict
summarize	categorize
rewrite	justify
criticize	paraphrase
operate	

and so on.

The kinds of behaviors teachers expect their students to demonstrate fall into three main types. These are cognitive or intellectual behaviors, affective behaviors, and psychomotor behaviors. Cognitive skills play the largest role in most instruction. This is where we are concerned with how students are thinking. Their thinking may be on relatively simple or complex levels. Simple thinking has to do with being able to remember and comprehend information.

The student will be able to spell correctly 80% of the words on the seventh grade spelling list.

More complex learning means the student is interacting with information at a more sophisticated level. For example, he may evaluate information or analyze or reconstruct it in some way.

The student will be able to predict the economic effects of a drought in California.

Most teachers find it easier to write objectives in terms of simple thinking, even though they frequently expect students to demonstrate more complex thinking skills.

A second type of behavior frequently found in objectives is called affective behavior. This area consists of actions which indicate how a student feels about something.

> The student nurse's behavior in the hospital will show a regard for the patient's right to privacy.
>
> *or*
>
> The student will show more interest in reading poetry.

These are the hardest objectives to write because of the difficulty in identifying just how a person feels.

The third type of behaviors found in objectives are the psychomotor behaviors. These are often the easiest objectives to write because by their very nature these behaviors are always observable. These are the action objectives.

> Using a mannequin, the student will be able to demonstrate a one-person rescue in a witnessed cardiac arrest.

When you write your objectives, they will fall into one of these three categories, cognitive, affective, or psychomotor. The behavioral aspect of your objectives is perhaps the most important part to specify clearly.

As stated earlier in this chapter, a well-written objective will also include statements about the conditions under which the student will perform the expected behaviors and the criteria by which they will be judged. It is only fair to the students to include this information. They need to know, for example, if they will be allowed to use calculators to solve their problems in statistics. Likewise, it is also only fair that they know beforehand that you will expect 100% proficiency on their test of medical abbreviations.

More and more teachers at all levels are structuring their courses around behavioral objectives. It is becoming second nature to them to think of their students' learning in terms of observable changes in behavior. In outlining their courses, these teachers have shifted their focus from the content to the students and their abilities to use that content. If, however, you are an instructor who is used to outlining your content and using that as a guide for your instruction, you may want to consider the following procedure for transforming this outline into learning objectives. Take your outline and at each point include a statement of how you expect your students to interact with that particular unit of content. Be sure to use action verbs which indicate behavior you will be able to either see or hear.

Industrial Revolution—Course Outline (partial)
I. Political and Social Thought in the Industrial Age Before Marx.
   A. Utilitarianism and Social Reform
   B. Saint Simonians and Christian Democrats
Student Behavior:
   - *Compare* utilitarianism to the 18th Century enlightenment.
   - *Identify* major ideas of Bentham's theory.
   - *Describe* the effects of utilitarianism on English law.
   - *Identify* major ideas of Saint Simonian's Utopianism.
   - *Analyze* relation of Utopianism to Fourier's and Owen's experiments.
   - *Describe* Fourier's and Owen's experiments.
   - *Compare* England's Christian Democrats to the experiments of Fourier and Owen.
   - *Show* increased interest in Utopian movements.

Next, add in any conditions and criteria which the student needs to know so he can successfully perform these behaviors.

> *Describe* Fourier's and Owen's experiments.
> Conditions and Criteria:
> - Refer to at least one outside reference.
> - Include at least the following points:
>   location, economic policies, governing policies, dates of existence, types of family units, and reasons for failure.

Whatever your final list of objectives looks like, you have completed the first step in designing your tests. Your list may represent a whole semester of instruction, and you may want to divide it into smaller, manageable units for the purpose of instruction and testing. You will need at least one test for each unit of instruction.

This is also a good time to categorize your objectives by behavior. Indicate whether they call for cognitive, or non-cognitive skills (either affective or psychomotor). As you will see, there are different types of tests which are appropriate for each type of behavior. The paper-pencil tests covered in the first six chapters of this book are the best tools for testing cognitive or intellectual skills. The remaining chapters cover methods of testing affective and psychomotor behaviors.

Now that you have divided them by behavior and type of test, you will probably note that some of these objectives are more *important* than others. An easy system for indicating which ones are more important is to assign a "1" to those that are least emphasized, a "2" to those of intermediate emphasis, and a "3" to those that are most important. When you design your test, you know that you will want to include three times as many questions for the "3" objectives as for the "1" objectives.

This outline (see Figure 2.1) will serve as a guide for your test. You know exactly what content and behaviors you want to test. You also know the relative proportions of questions to ask, depending on the importance of an objective. If you follow your outline of objectives when you design your test, you can be sure that your test is valid, that is, that it tests what it is intended to test. Using this system of outlining, you can avoid one of the common pitfalls into which many teachers fall. An example of a common mistake is the teacher who finds it easier to write questions for a certain topic and loads up the test with questions only in one or two areas. Another teacher may completely forget or, on the other hand, overemphasize certain parts of the course. A test that reflects a teacher's memory or special interests, rather than the objectives, is usually not a valid test.

You may find after teaching a unit that you did not follow your original guide precisely. You may have omitted certain topics or spent more time on others than you originally planned. It is only fair to change the test to more accurately reflect the relative emphases of the actual instruction.

With this basic test map before you, you can now move on to Chapter 3, which discusses the next step in writing your test. This next task is to write questions which accurately reflect each objective.

Chapter Summary

By giving time and careful thought to your objectives, you can practically guarantee the success of your tests. Tests are a natural outgrowth or extension of your objectives, particularly if the objectives are well-designed. The most useful objectives state clearly what you expect your students to learn, in addition to saying what the results look like when they have learned it. Knowing what you're looking for before sitting down to write a test will greatly reduce any problems

Figure 2.1

A Basic Test Map

In this unit on Animals and Humans, the sources
of information are the text (pages 25-47), class
discussions, and any outside reading the student
chooses to do. Based on this information the
student will: **Type of Test**

Week or Unit #	Objectives	Weight	Written	Performance
1	• Identify from lists and pictures:			
	Animals that give us food.	1	X	
	Animals that give us clothing.	1	X	
	Animals that are nocturnal.	1	X	
	Animals that are dangerous to humans.	1	X	
2	Habitats of selected animals.	1	X	
	Camouflage markings and behavior of selected animals.	1	X	
	• Identify the type of danger selected animals present to humans.	1	X	
	• Perform simulated first aid for snake bite.	2	X	X
	• Perform simulated first aid for dog bite.	2	X	X
3	• Research and describe the food chain of any wild animal (must include at least three links).	3	X	
4	• Argue for and against recreational hunting. (Arguments are presented orally, and must include at *least* the following points: environmental impact, supportive statistics, and man as master or servant.)	3		X
	• Make a personal stand for or against hunting.	0		X

in creating questions or situations which will allow your students to show you what they know.

If you are organized and systematic in planning your objectives and instruction, you can also save considerable time in designing tests. By developing a test map, as described in this chapter, you will have a handy reference which tells you what kinds of questions to ask, their relative importance, and even the general type of test you should design—either paper-pencil or performance. You can have confidence in the scores of tests based on a system of well-defined, well-organized objectives because you know that those scores are directly related to what you were teaching your students.

Chapter 3

Matching Test Questions
to Objectives

You now have a general idea of the content of your test as a whole. The next step is to start writing the individual questions. Chapters 4 and 5 give guidelines for writing these question in the most appropriate form, such as essay or multiple-choice. Before that, however, you want to make sure that the substance of the questions is correct.

The most important aspect of a test is that its questions truly ask students to show that they have learned what was taught them. Consider the following examples of a test item:

> You provide the students with a list of major actions taken by the British government which led up to the Revolutionary War. The question asks the students to draw a time line placing the events in correct chronological order. Which of the following objectives does this question most closely test?
>
> 1. Students will explain the cause-effect relationships between major pre-Revolutionary events and the outbreak of the Revolutionary War.

2. Students will recall the major events which preceded and precipitated the Revolutionary War and their dates.
3. Students will select the most significant events leading up to the Revolutionary War and justify the choice of those events.

All of the objectives are concerned with the events leading up to the Revolutionary War, so the test question is related to each objective to some extent. Beyond the general content area, however, the test question is clearly not related to Objective #1. That objective says the student will be able to *explain*. The test question does not give the student a chance to explain anything. Nor does the test question ask the student to select and justify, which are the two things Objective #3 says the student will be able to do.

Objective #2 is the closest match to the test question. But look again. The objective says the student will be able to recall certain events and dates. The test question provides the student with the list of events. They simply have to remember dates. The question only lists actions taken by the British government. You would not be able to use this question if you also wanted to find out if the student remembered major Colonial events and their dates.

This example makes it easy to see the discrepancies between objectives and the test questions that are supposed to show whether the student learned those objectives. In practice, however, it is harder to see these discrepancies. One reason is that many people write test questions without consulting the objectives or the content of the course. The criterion for a good question often seems to be one of the following:

- "This one will make them think!"
- "That sounds good."
- "I'll get 'em with this one!"

- "I think we covered this—anyway, they just *ought* to know it."

The result of this kind of test design is that the *content* you taught is usually covered pretty well. However, quite often the test questions are only coincidentally related to what you expected the students to *do* with that content.

The rest of this chapter will show you how to make *sure* your test questions are the best ones to ask in order to find out if the students learned what you intended them to learn.

As a general rule, every time you write a test question, ask yourself the following questions:

- "What is this question *intended* to measure?"
- "What is this question *really* measuring?"

More specifically, the following steps provide a way of matching the test questions to the course content and objectives. The procedure consists of comparing the behaviors you expect to see in your students with the behaviors your test questions ask them to demonstrate. Where there is a discrepancy, you make the necessary adjustments.

Step One: Analyze the Objective

Read one of your objectives. Identify the content this objective covers.

Objective: The student will name five or more animals that give us clothing.

Content: Animals that give us clothing.

Now identify how the student will interact with this content. In other words, what does the objective say the student will be able to *do*? It should be something you can see or hear.

> *Objective:* The student will name five or more animals
> that give us clothing.
> *Behavior:* Name (five or more)

Looking at your own objectives, you will probably see that identifying the content is not normally difficult. Identifying the behavior can be more complicated. Consider the following list of behaviors taken from some objectives:

"Write a rationale ... "
"Distinguish between ... "
"Draw a conclusion ... "
"Demonstrate (a skill) ... "
"Describe in a five-minute speech ... "

Most of these behaviors are straightforward. "Write a rationale," "describe in a five-minute speech," and "demonstrate a skill" are obvious behaviors. "Distinguish between" is like the oft-mentioned behavior "identify." There are many ways a student can demonstrate these "internal" behaviors, for example, by pointing to, circling, underlining, or stating aloud.

Identifying the behavior includes identifying the conditions under which it will occur. For example, consider "demonstrate a skill." *Where* will this be demonstrated? In the actual setting in which it is to be used, or in a simulated setting? Will the student receive prompting? What degree of proficiency do you expect? If your objective does not already include a statement of the conditions, jot them down.

In summary, then, there are three things to identify in your objective: the content, the behavior, and the conditions. The following example represents the whole process.

> *Objective:* Students will identify nocturnal animals
> from lists and pictures.

Content: Nocturnal animals.

Behavior: Identify (point to, circle, otherwise draw attention to).

Conditions: Using lists (of words) and pictures (graphic and photographic).

Step Two: Write the Question

Write at least one test question which you think will show that the student has learned the objective. Complicated objectives that cover a lot of content and many behaviors under a variety of conditions will need many test questions, of course. For the sake of example, however, we will only consider one question per objective.

Step Three: Analyze the Question

Apply the same analysis to the test question that you gave the objective in Step One. Specify the content, the behavior, and the conditions of the test question.

Test Question: Using the attached restaurant menu, circle the dinner that provides the most vitamin D.

Content: Foods that contain vitamin D.

Behavior: Identifying which combination of foods contain the most vitamin D. In order to make this identification, the student is identifying vitamin D foods and remembering the amounts of vitamin D these foods contain.

Conditions: An actual menu. The student may not refer to outside sources, such as tables listing the vitamin D content of food.

This step of analyzing the test question is very important. Writing a test question often takes so much thought and energy that one doesn't always take the additional time to see what the question is *really* asking.

Step Four: Compare the Question and the Objective

Now, compare the test question to the objective. Is the content the same? How about the behaviors and conditions? Using the test question in the example above, about vitamin D, which of the following objectives is it most closely testing?

1. Using real life and/or hypothetical examples, students will identify foods which contain vitamin D.

The test question assumes that the student can identify foods which contain vitamin D, but it doesn't actually ask for a demonstration of that ability. Objective #1, therefore, does not match the question in terms of behavior.

2. Students will select diets which provide the minimum daily requirement (M.D.R.) of vitamin D for children and adults. Students may refer to M.D.R. tables.

Objective #2 asks the student to compute amounts of vitamin D in various diets and to compare them to certain standards, a different behavior. The conditions are different, too, in that the objective allows the student to use reference materials.

3. From a list of alternatives, without reference to tables, students will select foods and/or meals which provide the most and/or least amounts of the vitamins and minerals discussed in the unit on nutrition.

The only difference between the test question and Objective #3 is that the question addresses only part of the content and only one of the behaviors mentioned. Just one vitamin is stated in the question, rather than all of those covered by the objective. Secondly, the student only has to identify foods with the *most* vitamin D, not the *least*.

Step Five: Revise the Question and/or the Objective

Where there is a discrepancy between your objective and the test question, it is usually easiest and wisest to revise the question. Revising the objective means revising the instruction. Sometimes you may find, however, that the test question asks the student to demonstrate what you really had in mind all along. Then you would be wiser to revise the objective so that it matches the test question.

Regardless of whether you decide to fix the objective or the question, your task is relatively simple. You know exactly at which points there hasn't been a match between content, behavior, and conditions. Continuing with the same example, about vitamin D, the following revisions could be made.

Objective #1: Using real life and/or hypothetical examples, students will identify foods which contain vitamin D.

Test Question: On the attached menu, check off all the foods that contain vitamin D.

Objective #2: Students will select diets which provide the minimum daily requirement (M.D.R.) of vitamin D for children and adults. Students may refer to M.D.R. tables.

Test Question: On the attached menu, check all the meals

which provide the minimum daily requirement of vitamin D for children. Do the
same for adults. (You may use the M.D.R.
table on page 27 of your text.)

Objective #3: From a list of alternatives, without reference to tables, students will select foods
and/or meals which provide the most and/
or least amounts of the vitamins and minerals discussed in the unit on nutrition.

Test
Question: Using the attached menu complete the
following chart. Indicate which meal contains the most and least amounts of each
vitamin and mineral listed below. Use M
to show most and L to show least. Vitamin A has been completed for you.

	Vitamin A	Vitamin C	Vitamin D	Iron	Calcium
Meal #1					
Meal #2	M				
Meal #3	L				

By following the procedure outlined in this chapter, you can
be confident that you are asking the right questions. On first
reading this procedure, it may seem to border on hair-split-
ting behavior. With a little practice, however, you will soon
internalize the steps and automatically look at your test questions with a more critical eye. In fact, you will find yourself
writing questions with this process in mind.

Chapter Summary

Step One: Identify the content, behavior, and conditions
specified by the objective.

Step Two: Write a test question for that objective.

Step Three: Identify the content, behavior, and conditions of the test question.

Step Four: Compare the objective with the test question, noting any discrepancies.

Step Five: Revise the question and/or objective until there is a match on all three points—content, behavior, and conditions.

Chapter 4

Essay and
Short Answer/Completion Questions

As Chapter 3 pointed out, the most important aspect of a test question is that it ask the student to demonstrate whether he has learned the objective. However, if a question is ambiguous, with directions that are difficult to understand or with clues that give away the answer, it can interfere with the test's ability to show whether the student has learned something or not. This brings us to the second most important aspect of a test, which is that its questions be technically well-designed.

The technical design of your questions can take many different forms. These next two chapters describe these forms, help you decide when to use them, and give you tips on how to write them well.

A test question either asks the student to provide an answer, or it asks him to choose an answer from a list of possibilities. Essay questions and short answer or completion questions are the two forms that ask the student to supply the answer. They will be discussed in this chapter. Matching exercises, true-false, and multiple-choice questions are the forms used for asking the student to select an answer. They will be discussed in Chapter 5.

Essay Questions

Description

The essay question is one of the types of questions which asks the student to supply an answer. It may be asked in such a way that the student is given complete freedom to express his ideas.

Discuss changing attitudes toward care of the aged.

More commonly, however, the essay question is asked in a way that restricts the student's response in some way. For instance, the question may limit the content area or the manner in which the student is to respond.

In no more than three pages, list changes in attitude by health professionals in the last 25 years toward the care of the aged in terms of home care. To what events or research developments do you attribute these changes in attitude?

Advantages

There are some advantages to using the essay question.

1. An essay question is the best way to assess a student's writing ability.
2. It is the only type of question that can measure verbal self-expression.
3. It is the best way to assess a student's ability to create, organize, synthesize, relate, and evaluate ideas.

4. The essay question can measure a student's global attack on a problem as well as his problem-solving skills.
5. It can be used to measure attitudes, values, and opinions.
6. It can be used effectively when an objective calls for the ability to *recall* rather than *recognize* information.
7. Essay questions are *relatively* easy to construct as compared to objective questions.
8. Students cannot guess the "right answer."
9. Essay questions are practical for use with small groups.
10. Essay tests can be good learning experiences.

Disadvantages

Generally speaking, the disadvantages of essay tests outweigh the advantages. These disadvantages center around the basic issues of test design—validity and reliability.

1. Because of their length, essay questions can sample only a limited number of course objectives.
2. Essay tests are not the best way to measure simple comprehension, rote memory of facts, or to answer "who, what, where, when" questions.
3. Scoring essay questions is extremely difficult, time-consuming, and unreliable.
4. Essay tests favor the verbally adept student.
5. Bluffing is common and not always easy to detect.

Design

When you decide that an essay question is the best type of question to use on a test, the following guidelines will maximize their effectiveness. The first set of guidelines will help you *design* good essay questions. The second set of guidelines, in the following section, will help improve your *scoring* of essay questions.

1. The student has a right to know exactly what you expect of him. Therefore, when writing essay questions, you want to make them as clear and unambiguous as possible. This usually requires a great deal of specificity and detailed, precise directions. For example, use descriptive words such as classify, interpret, compare, outline, and state the conclusion. Words such as discuss, tell about, explain, and cover the major points do not give the student a clear idea of what he is expected to do. Another way of establishing a clear framework for your students is to specify the content to which they should restrict their answers.

   - From the following list of Supreme Court decisions . . .
   - Using *King Lear* as an example . . .
   - Given the following economic conditions and indicators . . .

   Yet another way of establishing a clear framework for the student's response is to limit the time or number of pages and to state the amount of weight being given to each question.

2. Don't give the students a choice of questions, since this makes the scoring even more unreliable. If you really want to test a student's learning, why give him the option of not answering questions which test that learning?

3. Use a relatively large number of brief-answer (half-page) questions in order to adequately sample the objectives.

4. Whenever possible, present a novel situation.

Scoring

Just as important as designing an essay question well is the need for good scoring techniques. There are two major methods which can increase the reliability and fairness of scoring an essay test. These are the analytical method and the rating method.

When you score an essay question using the analytical method, you follow these steps:

1. Before giving the test, construct an ideal answer to each question.
2. Break each question down into its different parts and identify the major points you want covered by the students' answers. By doing this, you are making sure that other people, as well as yourself, will score all questions on the same basis. Assign points to each section, depending on the value you feel each deserves.
3. Read the students' responses and give points based on the scale you have designed.

The rating method of scoring follows slightly different steps:

1. Before giving the test, construct an ideal answer to each question.
2. Read the student's answer and classify it into one of three to five categories, such as poor, average, good.
3. Read and classify the responses once or twice more. Average the ratings.

Regardless of the method of scoring, there are several things you can do to increase the reliability of the scoring.

1. Before actually scoring the tests, pick a few answers at random to see how they compare to your ideal answer. If it turns out that these students are answering a different question than the one you thought

you wrote, change your criteria for a correct answer. Once you begin grading, however, do not change the criteria again.

2. Grade all papers anonymously so that you are not influenced by personalities.

3. Read all the students' responses to one question at the same time before moving on to the next question. This reduces the possibility of the "halo" effect, which occurs when your impression of a student's answers are influenced (either positively or negatively) by the answers he wrote to other questions on the test.

4. Score all answers to one question without interruption so that all students are exposed to a consistent mood or frame of mind. (You can see why essay tests are more suited to small classes!)

5. Provide comments and correct the students' errors so they have a basis for understanding their mistakes.

6. If you are evaluating the mechanics of expression, they should be scored separately from the content.

7. Determine a policy for how to score irrelevant or illegible responses. Generally it is recommended that students not be penalized, but that you should point out the irrelevancies and illegibilities to them.

Section Summary

As you can probably guess by now, essay questions are not always the best way to evaluate a student's learning. Restrict their use to those occasions when you want to evaluate a student's writing ability or complex thinking skills that can't be tested any other way. Give the student a clear understanding of what you expect him to do and keep the scoring as fair and objective as possible.

Short Answer/Completion Questions

Description

The second type of question that asks the student to provide the answer is the short answer or completion question. The student supplies a word, symbol, or short phrase in response to a question or to complete a statement.

What is the chemical notation for sulfuric acid? (H_2SO_4)
The chemical notation for sulfuric acid is   ($\underline{H_2SO_4}$)   .

Advantages

There are only a few advantages to using a short answer/completion question.

1. It is one of the easiest types of questions to construct.
2. It can easily be used to measure simple learning, such as recall of information.
3. Students cannot guess the answer or rely on partial knowledge.
4. Reliability and validity are increased (as compared to essay questions) because more objectives can be tested.
5. The short answer/completion question is the best way to check certain mathematical skills. For example, for testing computation skills or the ability to follow a formula, the student can't solve the problem by working backwards from a given solution.

Disadvantages

As with the essay question, the short answer/completion question is characterized more by its disadvantages.

1. They are very difficult and tedious to score. You frequently have to make decisions about partial answers

or about unexpected but correct (or partially correct) answers that result from a different interpretation of the question. Poor handwriting can interfere with the scoring, too.

2. The scope of information that this type of question can adequately test is limited to that which can be stated in a single word, symbol, or phrase.

3. It is almost impossible to design short answer/completion questions that evaluate complex learning, such as the ability to analyze or evaluate.

Design

For the times you choose to write this type of question, the following guidelines will make them more effective.

1. Write the question so that there is only one correct answer, which is short and definite. As will often happen anyway, students will come up with unexpected but true responses.

> *Poor:*   Sir Francis Drake was a(n) .... .
> *Better:* What was Sir Francis Drake's nationality? (English)

Some of the answers you would get from students for the first example might include "pirate, explorer, Englishman, great man."

2. Specify precisely the terms in which the student should answer. For example, do you want the month, the year, or the decade? Will you accept the name of the state, or do you want the city as well? Likewise, specify the mathematical units or degree of precision if computation or a mathematical answer is required.

> *Poor:*   When was the great stock market crash
> that marked the beginning of the Great
> Depression?
>
> *Better:*   In what month and year was the great
> stock market crash that marked the be-
> ginning of the Great Depression? (Octo-
> ber, 1929)

Failure to make these specifications can complicate
the scoring. It also makes it impossible to determine
whether a student has a different answer because he
hasn't learned the material or because he has a different interpretation of the type of answer that is
expected.

3. Don't remove statements verbatim from textbooks or
   other material. This encourages rote memorization.
   Furthermore, these statements are frequently ambiguous when taken out of context.
4. Avoid giving irrelevant clues which give the answer
   away or make it easier to guess. One example is using
   the words "a" or "an," which indicate whether the
   answer starts with a vowel or consonant. Another
   irrelevant clue is to make the blanks fit the length of
   the word or to match the number of words in the
   answer.
5. Each item should be independent of all the others.

> A. Compute the area of a rectangle which is
>   nine inches wide by four inches long.
> B. What are the dimensions of a square whose
>   area is the same as the rectangle in Question
>   A?

A student is penalized twice if he can't do the computation in Question A.

6. Omit only significant words, but be careful not to over-mutilate the statement.

> *Poor:*   The title of the only ... by Debussy
>   is ... .
>
> *Better:* The title of Debussy's only opera is
>   ("Pelleas et Melisande")   .

7. Whenever possible, put the blank at the end of the statement. Even better, use a direct question which calls for a short answer. Questions are usually less ambiguous than completion items.

Scoring

You can make short answer/completion questions easier to score by following the guidelines below.

1. List all the possible answers you will accept on your answer key before grading the tests and give equal credit for each. Let students know if spelling counts.
2. Give one point per blank, not per question.
3. Put all the blanks for the answers in a column along the edge of the page. This will make scoring faster and easier.

Section Summary

Short answer/completion questions are best used for testing recall of information that consists of a word, formula, or short phrase. They are not well-suited for testing complex thinking skills. A well-designed short answer/completion question is precise and unambiguous with only one correct answer.

Chapter Summary

Essay and short answer/completion questions are both relatively unsatisfactory types of questions because there is such a high element of subjectivity involved in scoring them. Furthermore, these questions are not usually the most efficient way of finding out how much a student has learned.

There are instances, however, when either type of question may be most appropriate. Essay questions are good for measuring a student's writing ability and verbal self-expression. Essay questions also allow a student to demonstrate certain types of complex thinking, such as synthesizing or organizing ideas. You can get valuable information about your students from essay questions when you restrict their use to those types of situations.

Short answer/completion questions are also occasionally the most appropriate type of question to use, particularly in math or science situations which call for formulas or numerical solutions, or at times when it is important that the student be able to recall rather than recognize simple facts.

The essence of both good essay questions and short answer questions is that they ask the student to demonstrate exactly what the objective says he should know and that they ask it in a manner that is easily and clearly understood by the student.

In Chapter 5, we will consider the alternatives to the essay and short answer questions, which can provide much more reliable, and therefore much more useful, information.

Chapter 5

True-False, Matching, Multiple-Choice Questions

Chapter 4 covered the technical aspects of writing questions which ask the student to provide an original answer. These questions were characterized by their low reliability and inefficiency. While they are relatively easy to write, they are time-consuming and frustrating to score.

This chapter presents the alternative to essay and short answer/completion questions. This alternative family of questions consists of true-false, matching, and multiple-choice questions, otherwise known as *objective* questions. These questions present the student with a list of possible answers. The student chooses the answers he thinks are correct. This chapter will first discuss the general characteristics of objective testing. Suggestions about designing the three specific types of objective questions will then be presented.

Objective Test Questions (All Types)

Description
As mentioned above, all forms of objective test questions

39

present the student with several possible answers. He makes a selection and his choice is compared to a previously prepared answer key.

Advantages

There are several important advantages to objective tests.
1. They can be used to test learning at any level, simple as well as complex.
2. They are easy to score, either by non-professionals or by machine.
3. Objective tests are efficient. Compared to essay or short answer tests, it takes less time for the student to answer more questions. This factor increases the test's reliability and validity because the test can cover more content at a greater depth. The result is a more complete picture of what the student has learned.
4. Students cannot bluff their way through an objective test.

Disadvantages

There are some disadvantages to objective testing, not all of which are insurmountable.
1. Objective tests are more difficult and time-consuming to design than essay or short answer tests.
2. They can encourage rote learning.
3. It is difficult to design questions which test complex learning.
4. Students often resort to guessing.

Design

Whichever specific form of objective question you decide to write, there are some general guidelines to follow which apply to all objective questions.
1. You want to give the student a fair chance to show

you what he has learned. Help him out by asking clear, uncomplicated questions. You can do this by using words which are precise and by avoiding complex or awkward word arrangements. Keep the reading level low in relation to the students you are testing.

Poor: Of the following reference materials commonly found in a public library, which one would you utilize in order to ascertain the title of Mark Twain's novels?

     A. *Reader's Guide*
     B. *Encyclopaedia Britannica*
     C. *Random House Dictionary*
     D. *Bartlett's Familiar Quotations*

Better: Which reference book would you use to find the titles of Mark Twain's novels?

     A. *Reader's Guide*
     B. *Encyclopaedia Britannica*
     C. *Random House Dictionary*
     D. *Bartlett's Familiar Quotations*

2. Test worthwhile content only. Avoid writing questions which are obvious, trivial, tricky, or meaningless. It seems that this would go without saying, but it is one of the most frequent complaints students make about objective tests.

3. Only use items with clearly correct answers, or with answers on which "experts" can agree.

4. Don't take statements directly from textbooks or other materials.

5. Avoid giving irrelevant clues to the answer. There are several ways test designers give away the answer.

(a) Avoid using a particular response pattern, such as TFTTFT or babcbd.

(b) Avoid making the correct answers consistently longer (or shorter) than the incorrect answers.

(c) Watch, too, that you don't use grammar which can also provide clues to the answer.

> *Poor:*   A newt is an example of a(n)
> 1. fishes.
> 2. amphibian.
> 3. reptiles.
> 4. birds.
>
> *Better:* Which group of vertebrates does the newt belong to?
> 1. Fishes
> <u>2.</u> Amphibians
> 3. Reptiles
> 4. Birds

(d) Be sure each item is independent of all the others. A common error is to include a question which provides a clue to another question later in the test.

> What does the pancreas secrete?
> 1. Pepsin
> 2. Rennin
> <u>3.</u> Insulin
> 4. Ptyalin
> When the pancreas does not produce enough insulin, which condition results?
> 1. Gallstones
> <u>2.</u> Diabetes

3. Jaundice
4. Peptic ulcer

The second question provides the answer to the first question. This occurs most often when questions are written at different times and placed in different parts of the test.

6. If you write a question based on an authority's views which are likely to be controversial or debatable, cite the authority.

> *Poor:*   Vitamin C will cure the common cold.
>   True   False
> *Better:* According to Linus Pauling, vitamin C will cure the common cold.
>   <u>True</u>   False

7. When you design the whole test, group each type of question together so students won't have to waste time adjusting to different thinking patterns. Write clear, explicit directions. Provide a method for students to mark their responses which is both easy to use and easy to score.

Section Summary

This section has presented an overview of objective test questions with general suggestions for improving their design. In addition to these rules of thumb, there are various ways of improving each specific type of objective question. These guidelines are presented in the sections below.

True-False Questions

Description

The true-false or alternate-choice question presents the stu-

dent with a statement which he decides is true or false, right
or wrong, or to which he responds yes or no.

The planet closest to the sun is Venus.
           True   False

There are many variations of the true-false item. Two of
these are described here.
   1. Cluster type true-false: You give the student an in-
      complete statement with several suggested comple-
      tions. The student marks each completion as true or
      false.

      Insects can be characterized by
        1. three distinct body parts.   True False
        2. cephalothorax.   True False
        3. six legs.   True False
        4. jointed antennae.   True False

   2. Correction type true-false: A question is presented
      with certain items underlined. The student decides
      whether the question is true or false and then corrects
      every item that is false.

    Huckleberry Finn was written by Henry James.
      True   False   (Mark Twain)

Advantages
   True-false   questions   have   the   following   uses   and
advantages:
   1. They can be designed rather quickly and are easy to
      score.
   2. They can usually be easily understood by students
      with limited reading skills.

3. They are the best type of question to use when there are only two alternative answers.
4. They can be used to test a large amount of content in a comparatively short amount of time.
5. True-false questions can be used to test
   (a) attitudes, beliefs, superstitions;
   (b) the ability to identify the correctness of statements of fact, principles, and definitions;
   (c) the ability to recognize cause and effect; and
   (d) the ability to recognize the difference between fact and opinion.

Disadvantages

In spite of the advantages listed above, true-false questions have some serious disadvantages.

1. They can rarely be used to test complex learning.
2. It is difficult to avoid writing true-false questions which aren't trivial, ambiguous, or open to misinterpretation.
3. True-false questions are not well-suited for content which doesn't have clear-cut right and wrong answers.
4. They have limited diagnostic value.
5. They encourage rote memorization.
6. Students find it easy to guess or cheat when they take true-false tests.
7. True-false questions are susceptible to a "response set," which is the pattern of responses a student makes when he doesn't know the answer, for example, always answering "false."

Design

The following suggestions are presented to help you avoid some of the disadvantages of true-false questions.

1. Be sure the statement or question you write is com-

pletely true or completely false. Avoid using complex sentences in which a dependent clause is false while the rest of the statement is true.

Poor: The spermatophytes, the largest group of species in the plant kingdom, includes the ferns.
            True   False

Better: The spermatophytes is the largest group of species in the plant kingdom.
            <u>True</u>   False

            The spermatophytes include the ferns.
            True   <u>False</u>

The first example contains a dependent clause which is true, while the rest of the statement is false. In fact, avoid using two statements in a single question at all, unless you are trying to show cause and effect.

2. Avoid using loaded words such as only, all, none, always, never, which usually indicate a false answer. Avoid using the words could, might, can, may, or generally, which usually indicate a true answer.

3. Avoid using qualitative words such as few, many, young, old, small, large, important, often, which are ambiguous. You will avoid many heated discussions by not using these words.

4. Avoid writing negative items.

Poor: In preparing a soufflé, it is incorrect not to have the ingredients at room temperature.
            True   False

> *Better:* When preparing a soufflé, ingredients
> should be at room temperature.
>
> <u>True</u>   False

5. About half the answers should be false, but avoid creating a pattern of answers.

Section Summary

You will get the most mileage from your true-false questions if you use them to measure the less complex learning of your students. They are best-suited to content areas which are precise and clear-cut.

Matching Exercises

Description

Another member of the objective test question family is the matching exercise. Two parallel columns of information are presented. The student matches each word, number, or symbol in one column with a word, sentence, or phrase in the other column. The items the student is trying to match are called premises (the left-hand column). The items he chooses from are called the responses. The directions usually state the basis on which matches are to be made.

> Column I lists several Russian novels. Match each with its author in Column II. Write the letter of each corresponding author on the accompanying answer sheet. Use each author's name only once.
>
> | I | II | |
> |---|---|---|
> | 1. *War and Peace* | A. Dostoevski | |
> | 2. *Taras Bulba* | B. Tolstoy | 1 = B |
> | | | 2 = D |
> | 3. *Crime and Punishment* | C. Turgenev | 3 = A |
> | 4. *The Silent Don* | D. Gogol | 4 = E |
> | | | 5 = C |
> | 5. *Fathers and Sons* | E. Sholokov | |

There are some common variations in the design of matching exercises. For example, you may have an unequal number of premises and responses, which makes answering more difficult. Another variation is to provide the option of using responses once, more than once, or not at all.

Advantages

Matching exercises can be useful test items for the following reasons:

1. They are relatively easy to construct and score.
2. They are compact and efficient; you can test a large amount of related material in a short period of time and space.
3. It is not as easy for students to guess as it is with true-false questions.
4. Matching exercises are best used with homogeneous subject matter to test students' ability to match terms, definitions, dates, events, cause and effects, and other matters involving simple relationships.

Disadvantages

There are some disadvantages to using matching exercises in your tests.

1. They encourage rote memorization on the student's part.
2. Their use is limited to testing homogeneous material.
3. It is difficult to design exercises which test complex thinking and learning.

Design

For those times you can use matching exercises to their best advantage, consider the following guidelines:

1. Use only logically related material in a single exercise. Each response should be a plausible answer for each premise.

Column I lists several common measurements. Match each with its equivalent in Column II. Mark your answers to the left of Column I. The answers in Column II can be used more than once.

Poor: I   II
. . .   (1)   2 cups   A. Quart
. . .   (2)   4 quarts   B. Kilogram
. . .   (3)   4 cups   C. Bushel
. . .   (4)   16 fluid ounces   D. Pint
                                                  E. Peck
                                                  F. Gallon

Better: I   II
(A).   (1)   2 cups   A. Pint
(C).   (2)   4 quarts   B. Quart
(B).   (3)   4 cups   C. Gallon
(A).   (4)   16 fluid ounces

This question is measuring the students' knowledge of liquid measurements and their equivalents. They will probably not even consider the dry measure vocabulary (bushel, peck, and kilogram) as possible answers.

2. Avoid using an equal number of responses and premises. This way the student's answers are not the result of a process of elimination.

3. The directions should tell the students the basis on which they are to make a match. The directions should also state whether a response can be used once, more than once, or not at all.

4. Arrange the exercise so the student can answer the question efficiently.

   (a) Arrange the responses in a logical order, such as alphabetical or numerical.

(b) Place the entire question on one page so the student doesn't waste time flipping back and forth between pages.

(c) Limit the number of items. Fifteen is sufficient for older students.

Section Summary

Matching exercises can be a very useful, efficient method of testing homogeneous material. With practice, you should be able to use this type of question to test more complex thinking, such as the ability to make predictions or to identify relationships within highly sophisticated material.

Multiple-Choice Questions

Description

The most versatile type of objective question is the multiple-choice question. In its standard format, it consists of a stem, which presents the problem, and a list of possible answers. The student selects the one correct or best answer from this list. The alternative answers are called distractors. Their function is to distract those students who are unsure of the correct answer.

There are many variations of this standard multiple-choice question. Some of the most common include the following:

1. Reverse multiple-choice: All but one of the suggested answers are correct.

2. Combined response: In addition to the stem, a list of options is presented. The suggested answers are different combinations of these options.

Which statements characterize the echinoderms?
1. They are all marine animals.
2. They have a single foot.
3. They include starfish, sea urchins, and brittle stars.
4. They include oysters, clams, and mussels.
5. They have both radial and bilateral symmetry.

A. 1, 2	C. 1, 5
B. 1, 3, 5	D. 2, 4

3. Analogy: Three parts of an analogy are given and the student chooses the fourth part from the suggested solutions.

Caterpillars are to butterflies as wrigglers are to
1. adults.
2. flies.
3. mosquitoes.
4. larvae.

Advantages

There are many advantages to using the multiple-choice question.

1. It is possible to design high-quality items which test even very complex learning.
2. Multiple-choice questions can be used to test material which is neither homogeneous nor clear-cut.
3. The multiple-choice question is usually less ambiguous or confusing than either true-false or matching questions.
4. Multiple-choice questions can provide valuable diagnostic information. By examining a student's incor-

rect answers, you can find clues about the nature of his misunderstandings.

5. Multiple-choice questions avoid the problem of response sets. That is, students don't have a tendency to prefer a particular response when they don't know the correct answer.

6. The effects of guessing are small as compared to true-false questions.

Disadvantages

Even though multiple-choice questions are the most highly recommended type of test question, there are some drawbacks to using them.

1. Of all the types of test questions, they are the most difficult and time-consuming questions to design well, partly because of the difficulty of writing effective distractors.

2. Multiple-choice questions take more time to answer than the other objective questions, so less material can be tested.

3. Students with low reading ability or limited experience taking tests have more difficulty answering multiple-choice questions.

Design

You will find it worth your while to perfect the skill of writing good multiple-choice questions. Consider the following guidelines when you design multiple-choice tests.

1. As we have seen before, the main factor in writing good multiple-choice questions is to use clear, unambiguous, precise language. The easiest way to write a clear item is to ask a direct question rather than present an incomplete statement as the stem.

2. If you do use an incomplete statement, include as

much information in the stem as possible. Make sure
the solutions come at the end of the statement, not at
the beginning or in the middle. This will save reading
time as well as printing space.

>*Poor:* The Industrial Revolution
>   A. caused an improvement in the stand-
>   ard of living primarily for coal
>   workers.
>   B. caused an increase in leisure time.
>   C. caused a decrease in emigration to
>   the United States.
>
>*Better:* Which social change was a result of the
>   Industrial Revolution?
>   A. An improvement in the standard of
>   living primarily for coal workers.
>   B. An increase in leisure time.
>   C. A decrease in emigration to the
>   United States.

3. The distractors should be homogeneous and highly
plausible to students who don't know the answer to
the question. If the distractors aren't reasonable to a
student who is in doubt, he may choose the correct
answer by default. Use four or five options, if possible,
unless there aren't that many plausible distractors.
4. Avoid giving irrelevant clues such as:
   (a) Logical or grammatical inconsistencies:

>*Poor:* What did Napoleon do after he was
>   exiled to St. Helena?
>   A. Wrote his memoirs.
>   B. The Battle of Trafalgar.
>   C. The Battle of Waterloo.

Better: What did Napoleon do after he was
exiled to St. Helena?

<u>A.</u> He wrote his memoirs.

B. He escaped and fought the Battle
of Waterloo.

C. He escaped and fought the Battle
of Trafalgar.

(b) Making the correct answer consistently different
from the distractors. For example, making the
answer longer, more detailed, or following a systematic pattern (a,b,d,a,b,d).

(c) Verbal associations between the stem and
alternatives.

Poor: The price the buyer pays for goods
is called the

1. cost.

2. selling price.

3. gross profit.

4. net profit.

Better: The amount the buyer pays for
goods is called the

1. cost.

<u>2.</u> selling price.

3. gross profit.

4. net profit.

(d) Overlapping distractors.

Which of the following play a role in
digestion?

1. Tonsils

2. Pancreas

3. Appendix
4. Large Intestine
    A. 1, 2, 4
    B. 2 only
    C. 2, 3, 4
    D. 2, 4

Since 2 is included in each of the options, the student will always select it. You have not learned whether he knows that the pancreas is involved in the digestive process.
Another example of overlapping distractors:

In the story of "Georgie Grows Up," Georgie was a young
1. boy.
2. lad.
3. son.
4. girl.

If the answer to this question is not girl, the student will be right no matter which of the other three options he chooses.

5. State questions and options positively. The only time you should use a negatively stated item is when it is critical to know what *not* to do. Underline "not" so the students see it.

In an unwitnessed cardiac arrest with no breathing or pulse, the rescuer should <u>not</u>
 <u>A.</u> give precordial thump.
 B. maintain 15:2 ratio.
 C. open the airway.
 D. give four initial quick breaths.

6. Use "none of the above" and "all of the above" sparingly. Use "none of the above" as an option only when it is necessary for the student to know that all the distractors are wrong.

> The second President of the United States was
> A. George Washington.
> B. James Monroe.
> C. Thomas Jefferson.
> D. James Madison.
> E. None of the above.

Note that since "E" is the correct answer, you still have not tested whether the student knows who was the second President. Using "all of the above" encourages guessing. In the following example, if the student knows that two of the options are correct, he automatically knows that "E" is the answer, even though he may be unsure of the other two options.

> Birds can be characterized by which of the following?
> A. They are warm-blooded.
> B. They breathe with lungs.
> C. They have four limbs.
> D. They have a four-chambered heart.
> E. All of the above.

The combined-response question (p. 50) avoids the problems of "all of the above."

Section Summary

Multiple-choice questions are the most versatile and most useful type of test question. While they are not as easy to design as many of the other types of questions, they can give you the best measurement of your students' learning.

Combination Questions:
The Interpretive Exercise

Description

The interpretive exercise is a unique test item which often combines many types of objective questions. An interpretive exercise presents some introductory material to the student, such as charts, graphs, or a short reading. The test consists of a series of questions which ask the student to interpret the material. The questions may be of the true-false, matching, or multiple-choice variety, or some variation as shown below:

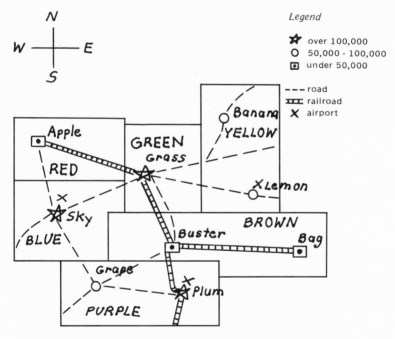

The country east of Green is
A. Yellow.
B. Brown.
C. Blue.
D. Red.

The southernmost country is
A. Brown.
B. Red.
C. Green.
<u>D. Purple.</u>
You can fly from Plum to Grass.
    True   <u>False</u>
You can drive from Bag to Buster.
    True   <u>False</u>
The northernmost railroad station is Apple.
    <u>True</u>   False

Column I lists towns which are *not* on the map. Match them to the countries in Column II that they should be in. You may use a country once, more than once, or not at all. Mark your answers to the left of Column I.

	I	II
(C)	1. Mint	A. Blue
(E)	2. Hot	B. Brown
(A)	3. Navy	C. Green
(A)	4. Baby	D. Purple
(F)	5. Chicken	E. Red
(C)	6. Lime	F. Yellow
(D)	7. Passion	

Advantages

The interpretive exercise can be an excellent type of question for the following reasons:

1. It can measure more complex learning than most of the other questions. Some examples of the types of learning it can test include measuring a student's ability to
   (a) apply principles;
   (b) identify cause-effect relationships;
   (c) identify unstated assumptions; and

(d) assess the relevance of an argument or adequacy of a procedure.
2. Interpretive exercises are an effective way of simulating a natural situation.
3. Interpretive exercises are challenging and many students enjoy them.

Disadvantages

There are some drawbacks to the interpretive exercise.
1. They are very difficult items to design. Part of the reason is that good materials are hard to find or need to be modified.
2. Interpretive exercises often place a heavy demand on a student's reading skills.

Design

When you write an interpretive exercise, follow the suggestions given for the three major types of objective questions presented in this chapter. In addition, the following guidelines will help you design effective interpretive exercises.
1. Choose the introductory material carefully. It should be brief, novel, creative, and on a non-demanding reading level. You may have to revise the material to fit your objectives and your students' abilities. While the material should be novel, don't make it *too* unfamiliar. For example, it would not be fair to present graphs if your students have never used graphs before. Finally, pictures or audio material should be of high quality.
2. The questions should be related only to the introductory material. The interpretive exercise is not meant to test the student's general knowledge. Rather, this exercise tests the student's ability to apply past learning to new material at complex levels.

3. Keep the number of questions proportional to the length of the introductory material. It is not an efficient use of testing time to ask the student to read a long paragraph and then answer only one or two questions.

Chapter Summary

As the saying goes, there is a time and place for everything. Each of the types of questions discussed in Chapters 4 and 5 is useful for some purpose. Figure 5.1 summarizes some of the major uses of each type of question.

The objective questions in general and the multiple-choice questions in particular are the most versatile types of questions. They also provide the most useful information.

You will increase the effectiveness of all your test questions not only by using them appropriately, but also by designing them well. A well-designed item is directly related to the objective and is stated in simple, clear terms that do not confuse or mislead the student.

Figure 5.1

	Best Used to Assess:	Not Best Choice for Assessing:
Essay	—creative thinking —global, integrative thinking —problem-solving —writing ability —self-expression —organizational skills	—simple recall (who, what, when, where)
Short Answer/ Completion	—simple recall only —knowledge of terminology, formulas, symbols, calculations	—any complex thinking —recall of informa- tion that cannot be stated in words, symbols, formulas
Objective (general)	—any simple and complex learning, depending on type	—creative, original thinking —writing ability, self-expression
Multiple-Choice	—simple and complex learning	
True-False	—knowledge of cause-effect —attitudes, superstitions, misconceptions —information with definitely correct answers	—complex learning, thinking
Matching	—associations and relation- ships within homogeneous material —definitions	—complex learning
Interpretive	—applying knowledge to new situations —evaluative thinking skills	—simple knowledge

Chapter 6

Making Tests Work

We have discussed how to make your tests reflect both overall course content and your specific objectives. We have looked at several suggestions for designing test questions so that they will be effective. Now we can take the first steps toward fitting these tests into an overall testing system which is efficient, systematic, useful, and fair.

Suppose you have written several excellent multiple-choice tests which relate perfectly to all your objectives. You will be wasting your time in giving these tests if your students can't read the test papers, or if you don't know how to use the results, or if you don't keep useful, accurate records. This chapter covers topics which will help you get the most out of your testing efforts. These topics include:

    (1) administering your tests fairly and efficiently;

    (2) cutting down on the time it takes to design and score tests; and

    (3) using test scores for making instructional decisions.

Administering the Test

The manner in which you present a test to your students

can affect their scores, sometimes drastically. You want to be able to rely on their test scores as an accurate reflection of what they have learned. Anything which interferes with their showing you what they have learned reduces the reliability of the final test score. You can't believe the score of a student who cheats any more than the score of a student who doesn't understand ambiguous test directions. The following suggestions are given to help you minimize those factors which interfere with the student being able to do his best on a test.

1. Everyone should be tested under the same conditions. These conditions should make it easier, not harder, to take the test. A few things which you can do to provide optimum conditions include eliminating distractions, such as noise or activity in the testing area. Be sure each student can easily see any exhibits you are using, and that he has adequate working space. You can't be absolutely sure that differences in scores reflect differences in learning if some students can see displays more easily or are distracted by activity in another part of the room. If you give the same test at different times, try to duplicate the testing conditions each time.

2. Another way of providing optimum testing conditions is to make sure the test itself is readable. Typed tests are easier for students to read than hand-written tests or questions on a chalkboard. Make good-quality copies. Students shouldn't have to waste their testing time trying to decipher blurred copies. Put all of the same types of questions together and provide a method of marking responses that is both easy for the students to use and for you to score.

3. All the students should receive the same instructions before answering the questions. Make sure these directions are clear. Any rules you make should apply

to all students equally. For example, if no one is allowed to ask questions during the testing period, then
enforce it for all the students.

4. Prepare your students mentally for tests. There will
always be test-anxious students, but you can do a lot
to minimize their anxiety. Remember that you want
to give them the best chance to show you what they
have learned. Springing "pop" quizzes or giving a test
immediately after an emotionally charged or physical-
ly exhausting kickball game does not give students
the best opportunity to demonstrate learning. The
best way you can prepare your students mentally is
to teach them how to take tests. Often, this is particularly true for adult students, who may not have
any experience in taking machine-scored tests. They
often score poorly because they waste valuable time
just figuring out the system. Let students practice answering questions similar in format to those you will
be asking on the test. If you do this frequently during
instruction time, your students can relax when they
see that the test is familiar—at least in terms of
format.

Making the Most of Your Time

One of the major reasons teachers design less-than-perfect
tests is that often there is not enough time to do a better job.
While testing will always be a time- and energy-consuming
activity, the suggestions in this section will help you use that
time more efficiently.

1. You can save time by writing your test questions
when you write your objectives. If you wait until the
evening before the test is to be given, you will have
forgotten many of your original objectives, and what
you meant by them. You also run the risk of writing

a test that you are not satisfied with, if you wait until the last possible minute. Aren't you wasting everyone's time by giving your students a test which may not give you meaningful results?

2. Keep a file of possible questions you may want to use on later tests. These may be rough-draft questions which occur to you while you are teaching that you can refine later. Make a note of the objective that the question is testing.

3. Share test questions and ideas with other teachers who have similar instructional objectives. If one of your colleagues is a prolific test question writer, you may want to exchange services. For example, you might teach his class a science unit while he writes a multiple-choice test for you.

4. If you have difficulty thinking up questions, go to your students for help. Use their wrong answers from homework or pre-tests as distractors. Or ask them to write sample test questions for the objectives. It can be a good way for them to learn the material. However, don't use their questions verbatim. Consider them a source of ideas and rewrite them if you decide to use them on a test.

5. You can save time over the long run if you test your tests. There are several ways you can do this:

   (a) Try out your test on a few students (from another class) or on a few colleagues. They will be able to point out confusing questions or directions. They will also be able to give you suggestions for improving the questions.

   (b) Keep track of how well your questions work. If you plan to use a test over and over again, you can improve it by revising or eliminating questions that don't work. For example, are there questions that most students never get right or wrong? Are there certain distractors that no one ever chooses? If so, they are not serving their function of distracting the poorer students from the correct answer. For a further discussion of item analysis, see Appendix C.

(c) Include experimental questions in a test. These are questions that you are testing so you can use them on future tests. Of course, you would not include the students' answers as part of their overall score. Their responses merely provide you with data which you can use to revise the questions.

6. You can minimize the time it takes to score tests by making them machine-readable or by having students or paraprofessionals score them for you. Whenever possible, turn over as much of the clerical record keeping as you can to someone else.

These suggestions are intended to help you use your time most efficiently so that you can afford to make testing one of your instructional priorities.

Using Tests to Make Instructional Decisions

You always want to have a reason for giving a test. In other words, you want to use the results in some way. Test scores provide the rationale for making instructional decisions. There are four major uses for tests:

1. *Placement testing.* You can use a test to measure what a student knows before beginning a unit of instruction. These tests are frequently called pre-tests. The placement test or pre-test gives you a baseline picture of the skills and knowledge a student already possesses. You may decide to modify your instruction based on this information, especially if your students indicate they already know what you plan to

teach them. You can also use the information from a placement test to rank or group students with similar skills and knowledge.

2. *Formative testing.* During the course of instruction, you often want to see how well the students are learning the material. You would give formative tests periodically throughout the unit you are teaching. These tests provide you with an idea of the effectiveness of your instruction. These tests also let the students know how well they are doing. This feedback is an effective method of helping students learn. Typically, a formative test will direct the student to some sort of alternative or remedial instruction if he is not progressing well.

3. *Diagnostic testing.* Some students may continue to do poorly in spite of remedial instruction. In order to pinpoint the exact nature of their misunderstandings, you may give them a diagnostic test. Such tests are usually very comprehensive and may require the services of a specialist.

4. *Summative testing.* You give a summative test at the end of an instructional unit. The information you get from these test scores represents a final statement about the effectiveness of your instruction. The scores from summative tests are most frequently used as a basis for assigning grades.

The type of test you decide to give can influence the types of questions you decide to ask. Keep in mind why you are giving the test, and use the test scores accordingly.

In addition to the reasons for giving a test, there are two ways of interpreting the test scores. These are known as norm-referenced testing and criterion-referenced testing.

1. *Norm-referenced.* When you compare a student's score to other students' scores, you are using a norm-

referenced measurement. With this method of inter-preting scores, you are able to rank students, showing who has performed the best or poorest. You can make a statement such as "This student is in the top ten percent of his class." Norm-referenced scores can be useful when you need to make decisions based on the differences among students. For example, you may want to select only a few top students for scholarships.

2. *Criterion-referenced.* On the other hand, you may only wish to know the extent to which a student has mastered a given task or objective. You are uncon-cerned with how his performance compares to that of other students. This interpretation of test scores is known as criterion-referenced measurement. You can make a statement such as "This student can spell 80 percent of the words in the spelling list and therefore has (or has not) mastered the material." There are many disagreements about what level of performance constitutes mastery. Since no scientific standard has been developed, mastery is exactly what you say it is. You may expect 100 percent correct or only 60 per-cent correct. One rule of thumb for establishing mas-tery levels is to determine the proficiency the stu-dents need to continue successfully onto the next unit.

You can see the difference between these two types of testing interpretations in the following example. Johnny's math score placed him in the top five percent of his class. While one would be inclined to give him a very high grade, there is no indication of how much math he knows. We only know that he knows more than 95 percent of the class. He may, in fact, know very little math. This is a norm-referenced interpretation of his math score.

Susie has correctly answered 90 percent of the items on her math test. Previously, her teacher had decided that any student who was able to answer correctly 75 percent of the questions could be considered to have mastered the material. We have no way of knowing from this criterion-referenced measurement how her performance compared to that of the other students in her class, but we do know that she has mastered the material.

Teachers usually use a combination of these two measurements, with more of a tendency toward the norm-referenced test. There has been an idea around in education for quite some time which says that something is wrong if everyone gets an A. Therefore, teachers try to rank students in comparison with each other, rather than in terms of how well they know the material. Actually, it would seem that teachers would be pleased if all their students were able to master the material. Why else do they come to school?

Either criterion- or norm-referenced tests can be used in any of the four testing situations, placement, formative, diagnostic, and summative, described earlier in this section. There are differences in the methods of designing questions for norm- or criterion-referenced tests, but they are beyond the scope of this book.

Chapter Summary

Testing involves more than just writing objectives and test questions. Tests only become useful when you give them to students. The manner in which you administer your tests can have a great effect on the students' scores. All students deserve an equal chance to show you under the best conditions possible exactly what they have learned.

Designing tests, however, can be very time-consuming. Careful planning and organization will save you valuable time and will contribute to the improved design of your tests.

Knowing what you are going to use your tests for can also help you become more efficient in your planning and designing of tests. This chapter has shown some ways in which tests can provide specific information which can be used to make judgments and decisions about a student's learning. Test scores are not the last word; rather, they are both the incentive and the guide for future instruction and learning.

Well-written objectives and test questions, careful test administration, a well-defined purpose for using the test scores, and efficient use of your time—these are the elements of a well-designed testing system.

Chapter 7

Measuring Performance, Products, and Attitudes

The previous chapters of this handbook discussed methods of testing cognitive or intellectual learning. Paper-pencil tests were shown to be the most efficient, reliable method of giving students an opportunity to show what they had learned. However, your objectives may include certain kinds of learning which are not "intellectual" in nature. For example, you may want your students to be able to perform a skill or procedure.

The student will be able to:
(a) make a cylinder key using the impression method;
(b) demonstrate the correct procedure for administering basic cardiopulmonary resuscitation (CPR) to a cardiac arrest victim; or
(c) process mail requests for season tickets.

Or, you may want your students to be able to create or construct a product.

The student will be able to:
(a) create a mobile with at least five branches;
(b) make a shirt with set-in sleeves, collar, buttonholes, and cuffs; or
(c) construct a circuit board demonstrating the basic principles of electricity.

Finally, you may be interested in behavior which indicates the presence of certain attitudes, values, or feelings.

The student will be able to:
(a) incorporate Maslow's hierarchy of needs into patient care;
(b) demonstrate consideration for peers, property, and the environment; or
(c) demonstrate increasing ability to initiate and follow through on class assignments without help from the teacher.

Obviously, a paper-pencil test will not give you a satisfactory answer as to whether or not your students have mastered these objectives. Your confidence in their ability will be increased if you actually *see them demonstrate* their mastery of the objectives. Ideally, you would like to see each student demonstrate a behavior, skill or procedure, or create a product in the most realistic setting possible. For example, you will have a much better idea of your student's ability to operate a cash register and make change in a busy department store than in a quiet classroom free of distractions. Many skills and behaviors, of course, can be observed in the regular classroom. For example, the school or classroom setting is ideal for observing and evaluating a student's leadership abilities, his social interaction skills, or his ability to use classroom resources and equipment.

Many times, however, there are objectives which the student should perform outside of the classroom. Unfortunately, most instructors and trainers do not have the time, space, energy, or money needed to observe students in real-life settings. Even when it is possible to observe students in natural surroundings, they may not act normally due to the anxiety caused by the presence of an evaluator. In situations involving human lives or expensive equipment, you may not want to risk testing students whose competence you doubt. Because of all these constraints on your evaluation of your students' non-cognitive learning, you will usually have to make compromises in the way you assess their performance. This chapter explains how to make rational compromises which will give you the most information possible within the bounds of your available resources. As with cognitive testing, your starting point is your list of objectives. Separate those objectives which can appropriately be tested by paper-pencil tests from those that require some demonstration of behavior or skill. (See Figure 7.1.)

Depending on your time, resources, and priorities, you may realize that it is impossible to evaluate every student on every objective in real-life settings. If this is the case, choose those objectives that for one reason or another you feel you as the instructor must see for yourself under realistic conditions in order to say the student has reached an acceptable level of proficiency. These may be objectives which involve risk to person or property. You would not feel safe about sending this student into the world unless you personally had verified his proficiency with respect to these objectives. Or they may simply be objectives which are especially important in your course of instruction and that you want to see first-hand.

Figure 7.1

Objectives	Method of Testing	
	Paper-Pencil	Demonstration
1. Describe signs and symptoms of hypoxia.	X	
2. Recognize signs and symptoms of hypoxia.		X
3. Describe the steps in clearing an obstructed airway.	X	
4. Demonstrate the procedure of clearing an obstructed airway.		X
5. Initiate and follow up patient teaching according to sound educational technique.		X
6. Start I.V. therapy according to physician's orders.		X

The objectives which are remaining should be those which you can afford to test under less-than-perfect conditions. They may be objectives which can be evaluated by someone else if you don't have time. They may be objectives which occur so rarely or unpredictably that you need to evaluate them under contrived conditions. For example, you cannot always wait for an emergency to occur to test the student's ability to respond appropriately to emergency situations. Or they may be objectives which you would reasonably expect the student to perform as well in real-life situations as he would in a simulated setting. For example, a student will

Figure 7.2

Objectives	Method of Testing		
	Paper-Pencil	Inter-mediate	Real-Life
1. Describe signs and symptoms of hypoxia.	X		
2. Recognize signs and symptoms of hypoxia.		X	
3. Describe the steps in clearing an obstructed airway.	X		
4. Demonstrate the procedure of clearing an obstructed airway.		X	
5. Initiate and follow up patient teaching according to sound educational technique.		X	
6. Start I.V. therapy according to physician's orders.			X

probably be able to repair a television set as well in a repair shop as he can in a classroom.

Figure 7.2 shows the list of the objectives used in the previous example. They are categorized according to the way a teacher might want to test them, by paper-pencil test, real-life demonstration, or some intermediate form of evaluation.

Categorizing your own objectives according to this scheme can be difficult because you are often deliberately compromising the ideals of valid, fair testing. Remember, however, that these compromises are eventually made anyway. This system of categorizing objectives allows for intelligent compromises which ensure that those objectives which *must* be seen in a realistic setting are not overlooked. One question you can ask yourself in regard to each objective is: "Must I actually *see* my students perform this objective in order to feel safe/confident about them performing it out in the real world?"

Test Settings

Whether you decide to test a student in natural, realistic settings or under controlled, simulated conditions, there are some ways of getting the most out of these testing situations.

Real-life Settings

The ideal setting for evaluating a student's skills, products, or attitudes is in natural, real-life surroundings. Some situations, however, are more "real-life" than others. For example, there may be many extraordinary or unusual events taking place during an evaluation which can affect the student's ability to perform at his best level. If the objective says the students will be able to demonstrate a skill, procedure, or attitude under "normal" conditions, then naturally you must try to assess them in settings which are as "normal" as possible.

Whatever setting the objective calls for, remember that the variability and unpredictability of real-life settings can interfere with the reliability of any measurement you make. Testing conditions will change every time you observe, which will affect students' performances. A student who is proficient under normal circumstances may make many mistakes in a setting full of distractions or other exceptions to what he is most familiar with. *Let your objective be your guide.* If it says the student is expected to perform in a calm, unharried setting, then evaluate him only in that kind of setting. On the other hand, if the objective calls for ability to perform well with distractions, interruptions, and emergencies, then you must evaluate him only under those conditions.

When you observe a student in natural settings, make a note of extraordinary or unusual circumstances which might affect the student's performance. Take those into consideration in your evaluation. If they are drastic enough to substantially interfere with the student's performance, consider holding another testing session.

Observation of Teller-Trainee
Unusual or extenuating circumstances:
- Computer was down twice for about ten minutes each.
- Two customers didn't speak English well.
- Trainee has just returned from three days of sick leave, which interrupted training.

Observation of Student Debate
Unusual or extenuating circumstances:
- Third day of heat wave, no air conditioning!
- Evaluator had only three hours sleep last night.

Contrived or Controlled Settings

You have probably decided that some objectives can be measured under less "natural" surroundings. You may also want to measure some of your critical objectives under controlled circumstances before you risk the possibility of a student's lack of proficiency in real-life situations. When you design these controlled situations, you want them to come as close as possible to approximating the conditions required by the objective. When you design a controlled testing environment, such as a skills lab or classroom mock-up, try and include as many factors as you can from the real-life counterpart. For example, if possible, have approximately the same space, identical equipment, the same time factors, and perhaps even the same types of distractions.

There are several ways of using controlled testing environments. For example, you may need to test a large number of students on a number of fairly simple tasks, such as their ability to perform a number of basic laboratory skills, including lighting a Bunsen burner, measuring liquids, viewing in a microscope, or operating safety equipment, such as fire extinguishers and fume hoods. If you have enough assistants, you can set up stations for each skill, with instructions for the students. Each evaluator monitors one station, evaluating the students as they come through.

Role-playing is another example of a controlled testing environment. Not only are role-playing exercises valuable as learning experiences, but also they provide excellent opportunities for evaluation. Create the situation and "character" in advance, and make sure you have all the supplies, equipment, or other "props" ready to use. One example of role-playing is to test young children's knowledge of emergency procedures, such as how and when to call the fire department, or police, or ambulance. Role-playing and simulated events are useful because they can be used over and over again. They can be made increasingly more complicated as the students learn more skills. For example, students posing as patients can simulate increasingly complicated conditions which call for more sophisticated skills on the part of the student doctor, nurse, or technician who is "treating" them.

There are many ways to be creative in simulating real-life conditions. Videotape and other audio-visuals are becoming increasingly popular. Specially designed equipment and models are available for a wide range of technical skills. Whatever situations you do create, remember that the objective is your guide for designing those settings. You want to come as close as possible to the specifications of the objective. Simulations can be fun to design, so often the evaluator loses sight of the purpose in mind. Keep asking yourself, "What is it I'm really looking for?" and "Is this setting designed to give the student the best chance to show me what I'm looking for?"

Methods of Observation

Now that you know what you want to see and the probable test settings, we need to look at the different ways of observing the performance you wish to record. The following methods of gathering data will be discussed:

- Direct observation
- Interview
- Self-report
- Peer review

Direct Observation

First-hand observation by the instructor provides the best information about a student's mastery of the objectives. You may choose to take a structured or non-structured approach when you observe your students.

Structured observations include one or more of the following elements:

(1) a statement of the specific objectives you want to measure;

(2) a tool for recording information you gather during the observation. This tool may range from the informal anecdotal notebook to a highly sophisticated rating scale (see Chapter 8 for a complete discussion of tools);

(3) scheduled observations. The student may or may not know this is an official evaluation session. You have planned this time in advance, however, because

you can reasonably expect certain behaviors to take place; or

(4) you have a particular student or students in mind that you plan to observe.

Unstructured observations, on the other hand, can be characterized in the following ways:

(1) you have no specific objectives in mind that you wish to focus on;

(2) your only tool for recording information is a blank paper;

(3) you may observe any number of students, depending on the events taking place during your observation; and

(4) the observation may be scheduled or impromptu. Students may or may not be aware of your presence or intent.

Direct observation is often the surest way to find out what a student can do. The next three methods, while valuable and appropriate in many situations, nonetheless are less reliable than first-hand, direct observation.

Interview

The interview is one of the best ways of finding out what happened in a situation you did not observe yourself. You can also use the interview to expand on your own first-hand observations by obtaining the student's ideas about what happened during the same situation.

As with direct observation, it is best to have a clear idea of what you want to find out in the interview. Your objectives will give you this clear idea. The interview consists of asking the student questions which will give you a definite idea of how well the student performed with respect to the objective. The trick is to ask questions which will give that information. Pinning down the student by asking for specific examples of behavior is the best way to recreate a situation. The example below shows these dynamics of interviewing.

Interview with Student Nurse

Objective: The student nurse will be able to describe given standard procedures to a patient according to guidelines found in course syllabus.

Teacher: This is the objective I'm interested in today. Summarize for me how you explain a technique or procedure to your patients.

Student: I tell them who I am, why I'm there. I make sure that we have privacy. Then I just tell them what's going to happen. I make sure they understand me and I try to make them feel comfortable. And I thank them when I'm done. Oh, and I ask them if they have any questions and tell them to call me or the nurse if they have questions later.

T: What do you do to insure privacy?

S: Well, I draw the curtain around the bed. If there are people around, I talk softly and move closer to the bed.

T: Show me what you say and do when you introduce yourself and explain why you're there.

S: Well, I walk in and—

T: No, show me. I'm a pre-surgery patient in bed and you're going to describe the general procedure.

S: OK. (Walks over to teacher.) Hello, I'm Ms. Jones, a student nurse. I'm here to describe what's going to happen before and after your surgery so you won't be worried. And see if you have any questions.

T: Give me some examples of patients that don't understand you, and what you do to remedy the situation.

S: Sometimes I have Spanish-speaking patients. I try to talk ... real ... slow ..., like this. I'm learning a few words, and I use them if they look confused, or if it's really bad, I go get someone else who can interpret. Sometimes I get old people who can't hear very well. I didn't used to notice because they'd just smile or nod at everything I said, but now I watch and see if they can hear me.

T: What about technical language?

S: What? Oh, well I guess I try not to use words they don't understand, but sometimes I forget what they don't know. Like some people don't know what I mean when I say they'll be getting an I.V.

(Interview continues with the teacher probing the student's answers for specific details that show whether the student's behavior meets the criteria of the objective.)

The major advantage of the interview is that it enables you to collect valuable data about an event you did not see. It also serves as an additional learning experience for the student. The more he becomes used to the idea of being cross-examined, the more aware he will become of his own behavior while it occurs.

A disadvantage to the interview is that often an articulate student can deceive an interviewer. The interviewer needs to be alert to verbal gymnastics which might mislead him into believing that the student possesses the abilities described in the objective.

Self-report

Students can learn to give remarkably accurate reports of their own behavior. This technique of gathering information, along with interviewing, is especially useful for dealing with those situations in which a student complains "but you never see me when I do it right!"

Self-reports are similar to interviews, except that no one is asking any questions. A student who is used to a good interview situation, however, will learn to internalize the types of focusing questions the interviewer asks. His self-reports will reflect his attention to these internalized questions.

The student needs to be familiar with the objectives if he is going to report his own behavior and his own progress in meeting those objectives.

Below is an example of a student's report on his own behavior.

Student Teacher Self-Report

Objective: The student teacher will be able to deal with unexpected classroom events in an educational manner and with a minimum of disruption.

Event: The class was doing quiet, independent reading and I was working with one student when the principal came in with two visitors to observe. Since the kids weren't doing anything that was interesting to watch, I had to think of something quickly. I stalled for time by introducing myself and chatting with the visitors (who turned out to be from the State Department of Education!). In those extra minutes, I decided to continue our class meeting we had started earlier in the day. I'm trying to teach the class group problem-solving skills through the use of a class meeting. We reviewed the problem we're trying to solve (how to raise money for a class trip to the Gold Rush Country). Even though we've just started working on this technique, the kids were great! Really well-behaved. Charlie even explained to them what our process is, what the rules are, and asked them if they'd like to contribute any money or suggestions.

Degree to which the Objective was met: Completely. There was *no* disruption and the solution was an educational activity.

Additional comments: It was a lot better than a month ago when the film projector broke and I couldn't think of anything to do except draw pictures or have another P.E. period.

Peer Review

One final method of gathering information is to ask students to observe each other and to report their observations. One major advantage to this technique, in addition to the fact that it saves you time, is that it can help offset the effects of your presence on the student's performance. Many students will perform better when freed of the anxiety caused by knowing they are being tested by the teacher. Another advantage to peer review is that students can learn a lot about how to do something by watching someone with whom they easily identify perform the same skill or behavior.

There are disadvantages, too, to peer review. A poorly thought out system of peer review can lead to some unpleasant classroom situations. The following guidelines will help eliminate or minimize the potential threats to classroom serenity.

1. Students should not judge, grade, or evaluate each other's performance. They should know that their only function in peer review is to gather objective data.

2. A student's grade should not be based solely on peer review information. You are still responsible for certifying a student's learning; peer review reports are just one source of supportive information.

3. Whenever student personal self-esteem or social relations appear to be jeopardized by peer review, you might consider dropping it as a means of collecting information.

4. Limit peer review to observing skills or products which are mostly objective in nature. For example, these situations would merely ask the reviewer for yes/no decisions, such as whether the student did all the steps in a procedure. Asking them to make decisions or judgments about the quality of a performance places an unfair responsibility on their shoulders.

Common Problems

Whichever method of gathering information you decide to use, whether it be direct observation, interviews, self-reports, or peer review, they all have some problems in common. Subjectivity is the major problem associated with each type of observation. As observers, we are all influenced by a variety of factors, such as our own physical and mental well-being, our feelings about the student and the task at hand, and environmental conditions, such as weather or noise and distraction, to mention a few. Naturally, all of these factors interfere with our ability to act as impartial observers. Thus, the statements we make about a student's competence are somewhat less than totally reliable.

There are some ways, however, of decreasing the influence of observer subjectivity. Some suggested methods are as follows:

1. Understanding the effect of internal and external conditions on your objectivity and being aware of their presence will help minimize subjective observations.

2. Practicing the skill of observing will help considerably. Choose only one thing to focus on in these practice sessions, such as one student or one type of behavior—for example, a student's verbal interactions with peers or his ability to follow a procedure. By focusing on single students or behaviors, you will learn to eliminate the effects of interfering distractions.

3. Be clear in your purpose for observing. If you know what you are evaluating, you will be able to concentrate on those aspects of the student's behavior without being overly influenced by extraneous or irrelevant behaviors or feelings on your part. You can also avoid confusion about what to record when you know exactly what you are looking for. Well-written objectives, of course, are your best guide in any observation session.

4. Whenever possible, postpone evaluation until after the observation. You can more easily train yourself to be objective if you don't allow judgmental thinking to be part of your observation.

5. Compile several records of observation from many sources, if possible, before making a firm statement about the student's competence.

Another problem that frequently accompanies observation is student anxiety. Quite often, this anxiety can have an adverse affect on a student's performance. You can minimize a student's anxiety in several ways:

1. Let him get used to being observed, by you and others. These observation sessions don't always need to be evaluation sessions. You can use them to provide the student with immediate feedback which will have no effect on his grade.

2. Allow the student to be part of the observation and evaluation process. Consider his self-reports and other input. This way, during an observation session he won't feel that he is really "on the spot" without any chance of his own perceptions being considered.

3. Consider the possibility of using peer observers. Quite often, students aren't as anxious or nervous in front of their friends and peers.

The observation methods described in this chapter have some drawbacks, namely subjectivity on the part of the observer and anxiety on the part of the student. Understanding and guarding against these problems will minimize their effect on the reliability of your evaluations. For the present time, they remain our best methods of gathering data about the nature of our students' non-cognitive learning.

Chapter Summary

This chapter has discussed methods of focusing exactly on what you want to evaluate. Starting with your course objectives, first decide whether you want to evaluate them by direct or secondhand observation, in a real-life or controlled situation. After you identify or design the setting(s) in which you will test the students, choose the method(s) for gathering information about the students' ability relative to each objective. You can gather this information through self-reports, interviews, peer reports, and your own observations.

Chapter 8

Tools for Measuring
Performance, Products, and Attitudes

The preceding chapter discussed how to decide what to evaluate, the setting in which to evaluate it, and how to gather your information. This chapter will discuss three different types of tools you can use to record your information. These tools are important because they relieve you of the task of having to remember lots of events and activities. More importantly, these tools organize your observations in ways which can minimize to some extent the effects of subjectivity on your evaluation.

The three tools we will consider are checklists, rating scales, and anecdotal notes. Each has its own particular advantages and disadvantages. This chapter will discuss these recording devices and will present suggestions and guidelines for designing each. Before examining these tools separately, however, let's first look at what they have in common.

The reference point for any evaluation tool is the objective. The beginning chapters of this book showed how this is true for paper-pencil tests. The same is true for non-cognitive evaluation. Well-defined, specific objectives, stated in terms of behavior you can see or hear, form the basis for any evaluation tool. Consider the following objectives:

- In a series of solos of increasing difficulty presented before the class, the vocal student will show overall improvement in tone quality, pitch, expression, and stage presence.
- The student will create a model of the planetary system which includes the sun, planets, moons, and paths of rotation.
- Over a three-month period, the student will show increasing interest in science, by spending more time at the Science Center, talking spontaneously about science activities, checking out science books, asking science-related questions, etc.

A well-stated objective will tell you and the students what you are looking for, and what you are grading them on. Objectives are the reference point for any recording tool. That is, whenever you design a recording tool, such as a checklist or rating scale, you use the objectives to provide the content for that tool.

Writing objectives in explicit, unambiguous, behavioral terms, to the extent that this is possible, will help counteract one of the major drawbacks of non-cognitive evaluation, namely, subjectivity. None of the tools discussed in this chapter is noted for high reliability primarily because of the effects of varying personal observations and judgment. To reiterate once again, have a good picture of exactly what you expect of your students, and know what that picture looks like and sounds like. Your evaluation tools then will become much more useful and meaningful.

Let us now look at the three tools—checklists, rating scales, and anecdotal notes.

Checklists

Description

The most usual form of a checklist is simply a list of all the separate actions that make up a given test. You check off those that occur during your observations of the student's performance of the task.

Checklist for Making a Soufflé

Student performs all of the following steps:

. . . Assemble equipment.*
. . . Assemble ingredients.*
. . . Preheat oven.*
. . . Separate eggs.
. . . Prepare mixture.
. . . Beat egg whites.
. . . Fold egg whites into mixture.
. . . Bake.
. . . Determine doneness.
. . . Serve.

*First three steps can be done in any order.

Checklists are also used for evaluating products which the student creates.

Checklist for "Ojo de Dios" (yarn craft)

. . . Four or more colors of yarn
. . . Proper tension in all windings
. . . No loose ends of yarn showing
. . . Equal windings
. . . Errors in wrapping not more than 1/4" off

. . . Ends of arms are finished off

. . . Loop for hanging

Advantages

Checklists are most useful for evaluating very routine, rote tasks which do not have many variations in the ways they can be performed. The checklist is best used for tasks which involve primarily psychomotor skills; they are difficult to use to evaluate behavior which must be inferred, such as problem-solving skills or judgment or organizational abilities. One of the major advantages of a checklist is that once it has been designed, it can be used over and over again by many people.

Disadvantages

Checklists are time-consuming to construct and can be difficult to use if they are too long or detailed. They are also not very useful in situations where you want to evaluate the *quality* of a behavior or skill.

Design

The core of a checklist is a series of questions or statements to which you can respond "yes" or "no." The student either did or did not perform each step in the task; or the product did or did not meet the specifications.

To design a checklist for a skill, start with the objective, which should tell you exactly what skill you want to evaluate, and what is the criterion for successful performance. Break down this skill into all the steps which the student must perform in order to complete the skill. This is called a task analysis.

> *Objective:* The student will be able to prepare a soufflé
> according to the procedure taught in the

cooking class. The student may choose the recipe.

Task Analysis for
Preparing a Soufflé

Assemble equipment.

Two small bowls for separating eggs	Electric beater
	Wooden spoons
Large bowl for egg whites	Measuring spoons
Soufflé dish (size depends on the recipe)	Saucepan

Other equipment depending on recipe: graters, can opener, knives, measuring cup, additional bowls. All equipment clean and dry.

Assemble ingredients.

Eggs—room temperature	Butter
Flour	Milk or cream
Others (depends on recipe)	

Preheat oven—according to recipe.

Separate eggs.

Break egg letting white fall into small bowl.

When all the white is in bowl, put yolk into another bowl.

Transfer white to large mixing bowl.

Prepare mixture.

Recipe serves as guide.

Beat egg whites.

Beat until stiff, but not dry.

Take 1/2 of egg whites with wooden spoon, place on mixture.

Stir thoroughly—slowly, lightly—one minute or less.

Take remaining half of egg whites, fold in lightly, slowly in up and down, circular motion—15-20 seconds.

Place in baking dish.
   Buttered or unbuttered depending on recipe.
   Place in shallow pan of hot water—if specified in
      recipe.
Bake for specified time.
   Open door five minutes before the time is up to
      inspect.
   Test for "doneness"—observe, shake gently.
   State reason for deciding doneness.
Serve immediately.

If you are designing a checklist to evaluate a product, list
all the attributes the product must have in order to be
acceptable.

Objective: "Display of States"
(Social Studies Group Project)
... All 50 states represented in some obviously logical
   order (e.g., date of admission, alphabetical, etc.).
... Each state's flag neatly displayed (drawing or
   photograph).
... Each state's flag and synopsis evenly placed on the
   background.
... Each state's synopsis includes following minimum
   information: name of state, capital, population, date
   of admission.
... Each state's synopsis presented neatly (printed or
   typed).
... Display is easy to read from a distance of three
   feet.
... Display can either be hung on wall or mounted on
   table.
... All information is accurate.
... Project completed by due date.

Items for Extra Credit
. . . Additional information about each state in synopsis.
. . . Use of additional visual materials.
. . . Exceptionally good lettering or drawing.

Your list of tasks or attributes may be so long that it is unusable. One solution is to edit the list so that it includes only the critical steps of the procedure. This edited list contains the minimum number of tasks the student must do to complete the skill successfully. Another solution for a list that is too long is to abbreviate each step. A more elaborate list can be kept elsewhere as a reference. This detailed reference list should be available to the students as well as the evaluator so they know the exact standards that are required of a successful performance or product. You can also use pictures or diagrams to illustrate exactly what you are looking for.

Checklist for Sterile Gloving

Steps	*Criteria*
. . . 1. Gets package of gloves.	Correct size
. . . 2. Washes hands.	See instructor manual.
. . . 3. Places package on clean, dry, uncluttered area.	
. . . 4. Opens package.	See instructor manual.
. . . 5. Puts on first glove.	See instructor manual.
. . . 6. Puts on second glove.	See instructor manual.
. . . 7. Keeps hands above contaminated field and in full view.	See instructor manual.
. . . 8. Recognizes and calls out any break in sterile technique. Restarts.	See instructor manual.

Note that each step is stated in such a way that only a "yes" or "no" answer can be made for each one.

The final step in designing a checklist is to determine the criterion for passing. The easiest system is to require 100 percent accuracy. Look at the example above for putting on sterilized gloves. The most important step is that the student knows when the sterile area has been contaminated. If you only required 85 percent proficiency in this procedure, the student could conceivably complete all of the steps except number 8 and still pass the test, even though the sterile field had been contaminated. It is less complicated to design a checklist which requires 100 percent accuracy for passing.

Section Summary

To summarize the steps in preparing a checklist:

1. Limit your use of the checklist to evaluating those skills, procedures, and products that are always performed the same way or produced to exact specifications.

2. Your objective will provide your starting point for the checklist. The objective should either contain or make reference to the criteria for successful mastery of the skill, procedure, or product in question.

3. Break down the procedure to all the steps it takes in order to be correctly performed. If you are evaluating a product, list all the attributes of that product you expect to find.

4. If the list is too long, edit it to include only the most important steps or those which are critical to the successful completion of the task or product.

5. Phrase each step or attribute in such a way that the evaluator can either say "yes" or "no" as to whether it happened. These steps may be abbreviated statements of more elaborate criteria which are stated elsewhere.
6. Determine the standard for passing. A level of 100 percent accuracy is recommended.

Rating Scales

Description

Rating scales are tools which allow you to record gradations of observation and judgment. Rather than being confined to "yes" or "no" statements, you can indicate the degree to which some behavior occurs or the quality of that behavior. Rating scales are best used to record observations of behaviors which are less predictable or precise than the skills or products measured by a checklist. They are best used for recording behaviors which reflect internal attitudes, interests, or values.

Examples of Behaviors Which Can
Be Measured by Rating Scales

- Consideration for peers
- Interviewing skills
- Interest in music (art, science-fiction, math, etc.)
- Courtesy to customers
- Public speaking abilities

Rating scales come in many shapes and sizes, however, they all provide a range of responses. The end points of the range or scale are usually opposites.

Strongly Disagree	Agree	Strongly Agree
Never	Sometimes	Always
Below Average	Average	Above Average

Advantages

Rating scales can be helpful recording devices because they are efficient. They specify your range of options for evaluating a performance, which saves you writing and thinking time. The information you collect from a rating scale can be easily tabulated and summarized. They are easy to read, understand, and fill out.

Disadvantages

Like any tool used to record and measure observations, rating scales are affected by subjectivity. The major disadvantage to their use, however, is that they are very difficult and time-consuming to design, if done with the necessary care.

Design

There are many types of rating scales; this chapter will describe only one. For more information on designing rating scales, consult this book's bibliography.

The more explicit a rating scale, the more reliable and useful it is to you. A rating scale which rates a student's performance as being "above average" or "below average" tells you little about the nature of his performance. The rating scale should give you an idea of how close the student has come to mastering the objective. Thus, the objective serves as the reference point. The first step in developing a scale is to "fine-tune" the objective. You do this by describing the minimum acceptable behavior, that is, the minimum behavior you will accept as an indication that the student has mastered the objective. Using this description as a reference point, next define behavior which is unacceptable and behavior which is exemplary.

Objective: The student nurse will demonstrate interviewing skills which (1) reflect consideration for the patient and (2) elicit the information being sought.

Minimum Acceptable Behavior Can Be Characterized as Follows:

- Student introduces himself.
- Explains purpose of interview.
- Ensures privacy.
- Asks questions in non-threatening, polite manner which the patient can understand.
- Asks all questions required by the form or procedure used in the interview.
- Records information accurately and legibly.

Unacceptable Behavior Can Be Characterized as Follows:

- Absence of any of the elements of minimum acceptable behavior (indicate which are absent).

Superior Behavior Can Be Characterized as Follows:

- Minimum acceptable behavior plus one or more of the following elements: Friendliness, ability to proceed under adverse circumstances, follow-ups on unusual or unexpected responses.

Objective: The student will be considerate of class-mates' personal belongings.

Minimum Acceptable Behavior Can Be Characterized as Follows:

- Student almost always remembers to ask to borrow classmates' personal belongings.
- Any damage to belongings is accidental—not the result of neglect or abuse.
- Student almost always remembers to return classmates' personal belongings.
- Lapses in the above are occasional and decrease over time.

Unacceptable Behavior Can Be Characterized as Follows:

- Absence of any of the above, which is not corrected after reprimand.

Superior Behavior Can Be Characterized as Follows:

- Minimum acceptable behavior plus the following elements: Doesn't need to be reminded to be considerate of classmates' belongings; helps others assume their responsibility.

While you will never be able to define behaviors so that they are completely unambiguous, that is the standard you are trying to approach. You want to try and describe the behavior you expect of your students in language both you and they understand. Using either objective in the examples above, if you were to simply say a student was "below average," without further elaboration, what would you or the student know about the real nature of his deficiency?

Each objective you describe in acceptable, unacceptable, and superior terms can be represented on a scale of either three or five points. A five-point scale offers the opportunity of making finer distinctions about a student's behavior. If you always use the middle point of the scale to indicate the minimum acceptable behavior, you will have a consistent reference point.

Unacceptable		Minimum		Superior
1	2	3	4	5

On a five-point scale you will always know that a 1 or a 2 indicates unacceptable behavior, while a 4 and 5 indicate superior behavior. In order to keep your scale down to a manageable size, you may wish to keep the descriptions of unacceptable, acceptable, and superior behaviors on a separate page. Below is an example of an objective measured by a rating scale.

Rating Scale: Citizenship

Note to Evaluator: Detailed descriptions of minimally acceptable, unacceptable, and superior performances can be found in the instructor's manual. Please review these before proceeding with the evaluation. Circle the number which best indicates your judgment of the student's performance. 3 = minimum acceptable behavior.

Objective: Student will show consideration for peers and for the classroom environment.

Considerate of others' personal belongings.	1 2 ③ 4 5
Considerate of others' feelings.	1 2 3 ④ 5
Respects others' privacy.	1 2 ③ 4 5
Takes care of classroom equipment and supplies.	1 2 3 4 ⑤
Adheres to classroom schedule and routine.	1 ② 3 4 5
Doesn't disrupt general classroom climate.	1 2 ③ 4 5

How you choose to grade this student is up to you. You may average the scores, counting a 3 as a C; you may weight the scores according to importance and then average them; you may fail the student for having been unacceptable in one area; or, you may let the record stand as it is without any grades. The choice is yours.

To summarize the design of a rating scale:

1. Begin with the objective you are evaluating.
2. Specify the minimum behavior you expect from a student who has mastered the objective. Be as objective and clear as possible, avoiding ambiguous descriptions whenever you can.
3. Describe unacceptable and superior performance with reference to your minimum standard.
4. Establish a three-point or five-point scale for each objective, using the middle point to designate the minimum acceptable behavior.

Section Summary

Rating scales are easier to use after the observation takes place or to summarize several observations which have been recorded in other ways, such as in anecdotal notes. Rating scales usually are not as specific or detailed as checklists. While they are time-consuming to design, and it is difficult to establish minimum levels of acceptable behavior, rating scales can be useful recording devices.

Anecdotal Notes

Description

Anecdotal notes are the observations you record in your own words. You may have decided to observe one or two specific behaviors in a student, such as his small-motor skills or his social interactions with peers. Or you may have decided to record whatever you see the student doing. The information you record is factual and non-judgmental. The evaluation of what you see comes later, after the observation period has ended.

Advantages

The major advantage to anecdotal notes is that no effort is required in designing them. They also allow for flexibility. If, for example, a student is not engaged in the activity or behavior you chose to observe, you can easily select another behavior or another student. Anecdotal notes can be a check for you in that they provide evidence which may contradict your general impressions of a student. Finally, they provide you with the most complete documentation of what you say happened, should anyone require a rationale for your evaluation of the student.

Disadvantages

The primary disadvantage to using anecdotal notes is that they are time-consuming and difficult to write. Unless you develop some shorthand system, you will find it difficult to record everything you see. Because anecdotal notes provide practically no structure, it is easy to lose sight of the objectives you are observing and evaluating. Thus, your conclusions about the student's learning may not be extremely valid or reliable.

Design

Designing the format for an anecdotal note is practically effortless. You need to record the student's name, date and time, and a general description of the context. If you are observing a specific behavior, indicate what that behavior is.

Date 4-6-78   Student   Charlie
Time 9:45 a.m.   Observer   Ms. Jones
Objective: (1) During independent study times, stu-

dents will use resources available to them in the classroom. (2) Students will be self-directed in their study.

Context: Independent study period; students working on term papers.

Observations:

9:45   15 min. after study period began, Charlie is walking around the room. Talks to George (1-2 min.), Bill (30 sec.), Kate (1 min.). Sits down at desk.

9:52   Looks in desk, pulls out books. Closes desk, opens, takes out pencil. Opens notebook. Stares out window.

10:00   Writes 1-2 words in notebook. Opens science book, looks at pictures.

10:07   Chooses page, starts to copy into notebook.

10:15   Gets copy of encyclopedia. Looks at pictures.

10:30   Selects page, starts to copy into notebook.

Evaluation: Uses his time inefficiently; very slow to settle down to a task, but is able to finally get to work, without anyone telling him to. Knows how to use encyclopedia.

There are several more suggestions for making the most of anecdotal records:

1. Observe and record enough of the situation to make the observation meaningful. Note any factors which might be influencing the student's behavior. For example, faulty equipment, crowded work space, extremes in weather, uncooperative patients or clients, or unexpected interruptions can all affect a student's performance and should be taken into consideration.

2. Keep the observations and the evaluation separate. It is difficult to observe a student objectively and judg-

mentally at the same time, so postpone making evaluative statements until after the observation is over.

3. Record both positive and negative incidents. There is often a tendency to record only the mistakes a student makes.

4. Write up the notes as soon as possible after the observation, if you are unable to write them during the incident itself.

5. Whenever possible, have several people submit reports about the student. Allow several reports by one or more observers to accumulate before drawing any conclusions about a student's behavior.

Section Summary

Even though they are time-consuming and inefficient to use, anecdotal notes are often the most useful of the three tools discussed in this chapter. They are adaptable to any situation, can be used on the spur of the moment, and don't require anything more elaborate than a notebook and pencil.

Combinations

There is no reason why you can't design forms that combine elements of each of the three tools. For example, you might combine a checklist with your anecdotal notes. If there are certain things you always look for in any observation, jot them down in checklist form.

Date	Student	
Time	Observer	

Appropriate Clothes:	*Work Space:*
. . . Safety glasses	. . . Tools in place
. . . Gloves	. . . Trash in basket
. . . Work shoes	. . . No unnecessary
. . . Apron or overalls	materials

> ... Everything cleaned
> up at end

Observations:

Another example of a combined tool is the checklist/rating scale. In addition to checking off whether the student completed all the steps of a procedure, you might want to rate certain aspects of the performance.

Checklist for Processing Membership Forms

... Greets client
... Asks for Membership Request Form
... Checks each answer on form
... Types membership card if   ... Refers client to
    all items are checked "yes"   manager if
    on form   there are any
... Returns card   "no" or incom-
... Gives client "New Member"   plete answers
    brochure   ... Thanks client
... Thanks client for coming   for coming
    Time Elapsed:

Rating Scale—Employee/Client Relations:

Rude, terse, slow/inefficient	Polite, respectful, efficient	Exceptionally friendly, extra personal touches
1	3	5

Rating Scale—Membership Card:

Messy, erroneous, or missing info	Mistakes are corrected neatly, correct info	No mistakes or omissions, correct info
1	3	5

Passing score = 100 percent, 3,3

Many variations are possible when you design tools for recording your observations. Whatever tools you decide to use, remember the following suggestions:

1. Use the objective as your guide for designing the tool. This will ensure that you are measuring what you intended to measure.
2. Be as precise and specific as possible, so that anyone else can understand and use your forms.
3. Don't put a great deal of energy into designing forms you won't use often. It simply isn't worth your time to design an elaborate rating scale or checklist that will only be used a few times or that will only give a very limited amount of information about your students.
4. You may want to let students use the checklists or even rating scales to study from or to test each other. They are especially valuable instructional tools because students know exactly what they are expected to do and what standards they are expected to meet.
5. Standardize your forms as much as possible so that other teachers can use them or so that you can use them year after year.
6. If you do decide to share your forms with other teachers, realize that there will never be unanimous agreement as to what constitutes acceptable behavior.

Chapter Summary

You will be able to use checklists, rating scales, and anecdotal notes extensively in your evaluation of students' behavior. As with any skill, it takes time and practice to learn to design them well. However, the alternative is to carry unspoken criteria in your head, which are so often inconsistently applied depending on the situation or on how you feel. These tools also spare you the necessity of having to remember countless episodes and events about each of your students. Should someone challenge your evaluation of a student's behavior or performance, these tools are a ready source of precise, detailed information. They are also useful tools for giving instructive feedback to your students about their strengths and weaknesses. As has been consistently shown throughout this book, the basis for well-designed performance evaluation tools is clearly defined objectives. The more you know what you are looking for, the less problem you will have in designing these tools.

Chapter 9

Putting Together a Measurement System

If you have been diligent in developing the tools described in this book, you may find yourself faced with mountains of unorganized data about each of your students. There's no way around it—testing can be a bookkeeping nightmare. Unless you have funds for an assistant to keep track of your data, there is no escaping the paperwork, except to give up testing altogether—an alternative which is not recommended.

This chapter will present several suggestions for managing and minimizing the record-keeping aspects of testing. If, after you read these suggestions, you find they do not fit your teaching style, by all means devise your own system. The key to your success, however, will be advance planning and organization.

In the long run, you can get the most out of your testing time and efforts if you create an overall system for monitoring your students' progress. In such a system, you will have a body of well-organized data which gives you and your students an accurate, developing picture of what they know and can do, and where they need additional instruction. One big step you can take toward creating order is to plan your entire testing program at the very beginning of your instruction. When you start drawing up your overall instructional plans and objectives, include your testing plans as well. These plans will consist of a schedule as well as a breakdown of what you expect to test at each testing session. You can even draft the tests at this time. All this advance preparation will not only save you hours of last-minute work, but also will ensure that you are testing your students on everything you are teaching.

There is often a logical order for testing your objectives. The most obvious order, of course, is to test them in the order that they're taught. Additionally, you might consider the advantages of "progressive" testing, such as moving from the theoretical to the applied. You can save yourself considerable time and energy if you plan to test a student's intellectual understanding of a skill before you test his performance of that skill, especially in those cases where life or property are involved. You might even consider an intermediate testing stage in a controlled environment before you test a student under normal, real-life conditions.

The theory underlying progressive testing is that it is highly unlikely that a student will be able to perform a skill if he doesn't already have in his head the knowledge needed to perform that skill. It does not, of course, always follow that just because his head knows how to do something, his hands will necessarily follow suit. If you have established this preliminary knowledge, however, you will not be wasting time asking the student to move on to the next step of demonstrating his ability to apply this knowledge.

Hopefully, your schedule will include lots of tests. You will find that by giving many small tests you will have a clearer idea of how well your students are doing than if you simply give one or two big tests a semester. The more mirrors on your students, the more accurate the picture, especially in the ambiguous areas, such as attitudes, values, and behavior. Whenever possible, collect and compile data from a wide variety of sources, including the results of paper-pencil tests, simulated testing, student self-reports, peer reports, and your own observations.

By testing frequently, your students will not only get used to taking tests, but also will learn from their mistakes. Tests thus become a part of the learning activities, rather than weapons or punishment for taking the class.

In addition to planning an overall testing schedule, which includes frequent and progressive testing, set up a record-keeping system which will show you and your students how well they are mastering the objectives. Once such a system is set up, you can easily teach someone else, such as the students themselves, to keep the records for you. Figures 9.1 and 9.2 show two examples of record-keeping.

Another suggestion for keeping order in your testing program is to correct tests as soon as possible, returning them to students immediately so they can learn from their mistakes while the material is still fresh in their minds. There is no reason why a test has to be seen as the final statement at the end of a learning activity. It can be seen as a springboard, bouncing the student back into the topic to learn even more. This will only happen, however, if you treat a test as if it is a learning device. Delays in correcting tests not only minimize their effectiveness as learning experiences, but also add to the paperwork problems created by testing. Somehow, one stack of uncorrected tests quickly becomes *two* stacks of uncorrected tests!

Finally, your students can help you by correcting their own tests and keeping their own records. Or, you may choose to ask a few students or an assistant to take over the task for the whole class. Even young children can be taught simple clerical skills. Cheating can be avoided by collecting the tests

Figure 9.1

In this unit on Animals and Humans, the sources of information are the text (pages 25-47), class discussions, and any outside reading the student chooses to do. Based on this information the student will:

Unit	Objective	Type of Test Written	Type of Test Perfor-mance	Final Written	Final Perfor-mance
#1	• Identify from lists and pictures:				
	Animals that give us food	X			
	Animals that give us clothing	X			
	Animals that are nocturnal	X			
	Animals that are dangerous to humans	X			
Criteria for Passing		75%			
#2	Habitats of selected animals	X			
	Camouflage marking and behavior of selected animals	X			
	• Identify the type of danger selected animals present to humans.	X			
	• Perform simulated first aid for snake bite.	X	X		X
	• Perform simulated first aid for dog bite.	X	X		X
Criteria for Passing		75%	100%		100%
#3	• Research and describe the food chain of any wild animal (must include at least three links).			X	
Criteria for Passing				30 points	
#4	• Argue for and against recreational hunting. (Arguments are presented orally, and must include at *least* the following points: —environmental impact —supportive statistics —man as master or servant)				X
	• Make a personal stand for or against hunting.				X
Criteria for Passing				30 points	
Criteria for Passing Final				60 points + 100%	

Figure 9.2

Animals and Humans
Student Test Record

	Geri	Bobby	Joe	Jane	
Unit 1 (Written)	78%=P	90%=P	65%=N/P	80%=P	
Unit 2 (Written) (Performance)	80%=P 100%=P	78%=P N/P	71%=N/P —	85%=P 100%=P	
Unit 3 (Written)					
Unit 4 (Performance)					
Final					

after students have had a chance to look them over and learn from their mistakes. If you have suspicions of falsified records, you can easily look at the original tests.

Chapter Summary

While the headaches of testing may never completely go away, you can do much to minimize the impact of all the paper and test scores and student records. Planning an overall testing schedule which includes frequent and progressive testing, creating a useful record-keeping system, and calling on your students to help you will all serve to pull your testing program together into a manageable activity.

It cannot be emphasized too strongly how important testing is. It is a vital part of instruction and deserves the careful planning you normally give to designing instruction itself. Being systematic, efficient, and organized certainly will make it easier to give testing the high priority it deserves.

Bibliography

Ahmann, J. Stanley, and Marvin D. Glock. *Evaluating Pupil Growth: Principles of Tests and Measurements.* Boston: Allyn and Bacon, Inc., 1975.

Anderson, Scarvia B., Samuel Ball, Richard T. Murphy, and Associates. *Encyclopedia of Educational Evaluation.* San Francisco: Jossey-Bass Publishers, 1975.

Bloom, Benjamin S. *et al. Taxonomy of Educational Objectives. Handbook I: Cognitive Domain.* New York: Longman, Inc., 1956.

Fitzpatrick, Robert, and Edward J. Morrison. "Performance and Product Evaluation." In Thorndike, Robert L., editor. *Educational Measurement.* Washington, D.C.: American Council on Education, 1971.

Green, John A. *Teacher-Made Tests.* New York: Harper and Row, 1963.

Gronlund, Norman. *Measurement and Evaluation.* New York: Macmillan Publishing Company, 1976.

Hauke, Robert N., Eugene R. Michaels, and Diana Welty. *The Design of Evaluation Instruments.* San Francisco: Far West Laboratory of Educational Research and Development, 1972.

Hodgkinson, Harold, Julie Herst, and Howard Levine. *Improving and Assessing Performance: Evaluation in Higher Education*. Berkeley: Center for Research and Development in Higher Education, 1975.

Mager, Robert F. *Preparing Instructional Objectives*. Palo Alto: Fearon Publishers, 1962.

Making the Classroom Test: A Guide for Teachers. Princeton: Educational Testing Service, 1969.

Mehrens, William, and Irvine J. Lehmann. *Measurement and Evaluation in Education and Psychology*. New York: Holt, Rinehart, and Winston, 1973.

Miller, Harry G. *et al. Beyond Facts: Objective Ways to Measure Thinking*. Englewood Cliffs, New Jersey: Educational Technology Publications, 1978.

Multiple-Choice Questions: A Close Look. Princeton: Educational Testing Service, 1963.

Payne, David. *The Specification and Measurement of Learning Outcomes*. Waltham, Massachusetts: Xerox College Publishing Company, 1968.

Popham, W. James, editor. *Criterion-Referenced Measurement: An Introduction*. Englewood Cliffs, New Jersey: Educational Technology Publications, 1971.

Popham, W. James. *An Evaluation Guidebook*. Los Angeles: The Instructional Objectives Exchange, 1972.

Popham, W. James. *Educational Evaluation*. Englewood Cliffs, New Jersey: Prentice-Hall, Inc., 1975.

Rahmlow, Harold F., and Kathryn K. Woodley. *Objectives-Based Testing: A Guide to Effective Test Development*. Englewood Cliffs, New Jersey: Educational Technology Publications, 1979.

Sanders, James R., and Thomas P. Sachse, editors. *Problems and Potentials of Applied Performance Testing: Proceedings of the National Conference on the Future of*

Applied Performance Testing. Portland, Oregon: Northwest Regional Educational Laboratory, 1975.

Sax, Gilbert. *Principles of Educational Measurement and Evaluation*. Belmont, California: Wadsworth Publishing Company, 1974.

Shields, Mary R. *The Use of Tests in Schools of Nursing: The Construction and Use of Teacher-Made Tests, Pamphlet #5*. New York: National League for Nursing, 1965.

Tuckman, Bruce W. *Measuring Educational Outcomes: Fundamentals of Testing*. New York: Harcourt Brace Jovanovich, 1975.

Wesman, A. G. "Writing the Test Item." In Thorndike, Robert L., editor, *Educational Measurement*. Washington, D.C.: American Council on Education, 1971.

Appendix A

	Recommended Uses for Each Item Type	
	Best Used to Assess:	Not Best Choice for Assessing:
Essay	—creative thinking —global, integrative thinking —problem-solving —writing ability —self-expression —organizational skills	—simple recall (who, what, when, where)
Short Answer/ Completion	—simple recall only —knowledge of terminology, formulas, symbols, calculations	—any complex thinking —recall of information that cannot be stated in words, symbols, formulas
Objective (general)	—any simple and complex learning, depending on type	—creative, original thinking —writing ability, self-expression
Multiple-Choice	—simple and complex learning	
True-False	—knowledge of cause-effect —attitudes, superstitions, misconceptions —information with definitely correct answers	—complex learning, thinking
Matching	—associations and relationships within homogeneous material —definitions	—complex learning
Interpretive	—applying knowledge to new situations —evaluative thinking skills	—simple knowledge

Appendix B
Checklists for Test Design

Checklist for Writing Objectives

. . . 1. Are the objectives stated in terms which specify the behavior expected of the student?

. . . 2. Are the conditions under which this behavior is to be demonstrated clearly specified?

. . . 3. Are the criteria for satisfactory performance stated?

Checklist for Designing Essay Questions

. . . 1. Is this the best type of question to find out if the student has mastered the objective?

. . . 2. Does each question ask the student to demonstrate exactly what the objective says he should be able to do?

. . . 3. Is each question clear and unambiguous so that the student knows exactly how to answer?

. . . 4. Are there enough questions to adequately sample the objectives?

. . . 5. Are all students expected to answer the same questions?

. . . 6. Is there a model answer written for each question?

. . . 7. Are all the papers graded anonymously?

. . . 8. Are all the responses to the same question read without interruption?

. . . 9. Are students provided meaningful feedback about their answers?

. . . 10. Are the mechanics of expression graded separately from the content?

Checklist for Designing Short Answer/Completion Questions

. . . 1. Is this the best type of question to find out if the student has mastered the objective?

. . . 2. Does each question ask the student to demonstrate exactly what the objective says he should be able to do?

. . . 3. Is there only one short, definitely correct answer to each question?

. . . 4. Are the terms (e.g., metric units, year, degree of precision) clearly specified?

. . . 5. Is each question clear and unambiguous?

. . . 6. Are irrelevant (e.g., grammatical clues, length or number of blanks) clues to the answer avoided?

. . . 7. Is each item separate and independent of all other items?

. . . 8. Are only significant words omitted?

. . . 9. Is the blank at the end of each question?

. . . 10. Is there a list of all the possible acceptable answers included in the answer key?

. . . 11. Is there one point per blank?

. . . 12. Is there a system for writing answers that is easy for the student to use and also easy to score?

Checklist for Designing Objective Tests, General

... 1. Is each question clear, uncomplicated, and easy to read?

... 2. Are tricky, obvious, or irrelevant questions avoided?

... 3. Is there a clearly correct answer for each question to which "the experts" would agree?

... 4. Is each item separate and independent from the rest of the items?

... 5. Are irrelevant (e.g., grammatical clues, obvious patterns of answers) clues to the answer avoided?

... 6. Are authorities cited in controversial or debatable questions?

... 7. Are similar item types grouped together?

... 8. Are the directions for answering questions clear?

... 9. Is there a scoring key?

Checklist for Designing True-False Questions
(see also Objective Tests, General)

... 1. Is this the best type of question to find out if the student has mastered the objective?

... 2. Does each question ask the student to demonstrate exactly what the objective says he should be able to do?

... 3. Is each statement either completely true or completely false?

... 4. Are loaded words (e.g., only, always, never, generally, could) which would give the answer away avoided?

... 5. Is each item stated positively?

... 6. Are qualitative or otherwise ambiguous words (e.g., few, many, large, small, important) avoided?

... 7. Are approximately half the answers true?

Checklist for Designing Matching Exercises
(see also Objective Tests, General)
. . . 1. Is this the best type of question to find out if the student has mastered the objective?
. . . 2. Does each question ask the student to demonstrate exactly what the objective says he should be able to do?
. . . 3. Is each response a plausible answer for each premise?
. . . 4. Are the responses arranged in a systematic order all on one page?
. . . 5. Do the directions clearly tell the student the basis on which he is to make the match?
. . . 6. Do the directions tell whether a response can be used more than once?
. . . 7. Are there an unequal number of premises and responses?
. . . 8. Is the question arranged so that the student can mark answers easily and so the test can be scored efficiently?
. . . 9. Are there a reasonable number of items for the ability of the group?

Checklist for Designing Multiple-Choice Questions
(see also Objective Tests, General)
. . . 1. Is this the best type of question to find out if the student has mastered the objective?
. . . 2. Does each question ask the student to demonstrate exactly what the objective says he should be able to do?
. . . 3. Is the language clear, unambiguous, and precise in each question?
. . . 4. Is as much information as possible included in the stem, with the options coming after the stem?
. . . 5. Are the distractors homogeneous and highly plausible?

... 6. Are irrelevant clues avoided? (e.g., logical or grammatical inconsistencies, correct answers which are consistently different, verbal associations between stem and alternatives, overlapping distractors)

... 7. Is each item stated positively, unless the intent is to test knowledge of what *not* to do?

... 8. Are "none of the above" or "all of the above" used wisely?

Checklist for Designing Interpretive Exercises
(see also Objective Tests, General and Specific Item Types)

... 1. Is this the best type of question to find out if the student has mastered the objective?

... 2. Does the exercise ask the student to demonstrate exactly what the objective says he should be able to do?

... 3. Is the introductory material appropriate to the reading level and experience level of the students?

... 4. Are the questions related only to the introductory material rather than to general knowledge?

... 5. Are there enough questions in relation to the length and difficulty of the introductory material?

Checklist for Designing the Overall Test

... 1. Are there questions for all the objectives supposedly covered by this test?

... 2. Do all the questions provide the student the best opportunity to show the extent to which he has mastered the objectives?

... 3. Does each question really measure what it is designed to measure?

... 4. Is this test easy for the student to read and use?

... 5. Are the directions clear, easy to follow, and consistent for all students?

... 6. Is this test designed so it is easy to score?

. . . 7. Can this test be completed by the student in the al-
       lotted time?
. . . 8. Will this test be administered under optimum condi-
       tions for all students?
. . . 9. Is the format familiar to students?

Checklist for Designing Checklists
. . . 1. Is this the best tool for recording observations of
       students with respect to the objective?
. . . 2. Does it include or refer to the behavior, conditions,
       and criteria specified in the objective?
. . . 3. Are all the critical steps/attributes included?
. . . 4. Can each statement be answered by only a yes or a
       no?
. . . 5. Are the steps listed in logical order that is easy to
       follow?
. . . 6. Is there a statement of the standard (e.g., 100 percent
       accuracy) for passing?
. . . 7. Has space been provided for comments?
. . . 8. Can this checklist be easily used by other instructors?

Checklist for Designing Rating Scales
. . . 1. Is this the best tool for recording observations of
       students with respect to the objective?
. . . 2. Does it include or refer to the behavior, conditions,
       and criteria specified in the objective?
. . . 3. Is there a clear statement of behaviors that are mini-
       mally acceptable, unacceptable, and superior?
. . . 4. Does the midpoint of the scale indicate the minimum
       acceptable behavior?
. . . 5. Has space been provided for comments?
. . . 6. Can this rating scale be used by other instructors?

Checklist for Designing Anecdotal Notes

... 1. Is this the best tool for recording observations of students with respect to the objective?

... 2. Does it include or refer to the behavior, conditions, and criteria specified in the objective?

... 3. Is it easy for the evaluator to use?

... 4. Will the evaluation be separate from the observation?

Appendix C
Item Analysis

One way to improve your tests is to analyze which questions are *working* and which ones aren't. That is, you want to keep those questions which identify the students that have learned the material. Questions can fall into any of the following groups:

(1) questions which everyone always misses;
(2) questions which no one ever misses;
(3) questions which high-scoring students miss and low-scoring students get right; or
(4) questions which high-scoring students get right and low-scoring students get wrong.

You can look over your range of test scores and get a general idea about which group your individual questions fall into. Or you can make a more formal analysis, which is described in this appendix.

Difficulty Level of a Test Item

If ten of your students take a test and two of them answer a given question correctly, we can say the difficulty level of this question is 20 percent. A question with a difficulty level of 30 percent or below is referred to as a *high* difficulty item because so few students were able to answer it. On the other hand, a question with a difficulty level of 70 percent or above is a *low* difficulty item because at least seven out of ten could answer it correctly.

A low difficulty level is not necessarily a situation you want to avoid. You may have taught the subject so well that most of your students learned it. On the other hand, a low difficulty level can also indicate that the question is too easy —almost anyone could have gotten the answer without studying.

One way to check out if the item is too easy is to give a *pre-test* before instruction. Compute the difficulty level for each question. Compare these levels to the difficulty levels of the same questions on the post-test, which you give to the students after instruction.

Item	Difficulty Level		Significance
	Pre-Test	Post-Test	
1	10	20	—not many students learned from instruction
2	80	85	—students probably already knew the material before
3	70	30	—something in the instruction is confusing them or the item is poorly written
4	15	90	—instruction has paid off

Discrimination Index

Item #3, in the example above, points up the question of whether students made a poor showing because the test question was poorly written or because the instruction needs revision. The *discrimination index* tells you how the results of a single question compare to the results of the entire test. If, for example, the results of a single item are about the same for the entire test, that item is said to be positively discriminating. If only the high-scoring students answer a given item correctly, that question is discriminating positively. Another way of looking at it is to say that an item is positively discriminating if only the low-scorers miss it. If all or most of this same group of high-scorers misses a certain item which the low-scorers get right, the question is discriminating negatively. That is, the question is separating the high-scorers from the low-scorers, but in a negative way.

It is possible to calculate the discrimination index, which can range from –100 percent (perfect disagreement, e.g., only high-scorers missing a certain item) to 100 percent (perfect agreement, e.g., only high-scorers getting an item right).

How to Calculate the
Discrimination Index of an Item

1. Rank students' test scores from highest to lowest.
2. Select top 20 percent and lowest 20 percent students. There should be an equal number in each group.
3. Compute number of students in top-scoring group who answered the item correctly. Do the same for the low-scoring group.
4. Subtract the low-scoring group percentage from the high-scoring group percentage. The difference is the discrimination index for the test question.

Students	Test Items (X = answered correctly) 1	2	3	4	5	Test Score
A	X		X	X	X	80%
B	X		X	X		60%
C	X			X	X	60%
X		X	X			40%
Y			X	X		40%
Z		X				20%
Top Group	100%	0%	67%	100%	67%	
Low Group	0%	67%	67%	33%	0%	
Discrimination Index	1.00	-.67	0	.67	.67	
Difficulty Level	50	33	67	67	33	

When to Revise a Question

Items with difficulty levels below 30 percent or above 70 percent (highly difficult and easy) will not have a high discrimination index. Items with difficulty levels between 30 percent and 70 percent should have a high discrimination index (above 30 percent). When these situations do not occur, you probably should revise your test item.

Difficulty	Discrimination	Significance
below 30%	low (below .30) high (above .30)	OK won't occur
above 70%	low (below .30) high (above .30)	OK won't occur
between 30% - 70%	low (below .30) high (above .30)	revise OK

Items with negative discrimination indexes should be revised as well.

Summary

Item analysis can be helpful to you, especially if you do a good deal of testing with a large number of students. Computers are ideal tools for simplifying this process as they can provide you with immediate information, freeing you from hours of time in clerical tasks.

Appendix D
Sample Objectives
and Tests

The objectives and tests in this appendix exemplify the major points made throughout the book. The subject of *locksmithing* was chosen as an example because it includes cognitive, psychomotor, and affective learning skills. An example of each major type of test and test question covered in this book is included.

By showing an entire unit of objectives and the tests designed to measure them, this appendix pulls together into a realistic whole all the elements of test design. The contents of the appendix include:

1. Unit Objectives
2. Test Blueprint
3. Tests and Answer Keys:
    A. Written Test #1 (Objective Test) and Answer Key
    B. Performance Test #1 (Checklist, Rating Scale, Student Record Sheet)
    C. Written Test #2 (Essay Test) and Answer Key

D.Performance Test #2 (Instructions, Rating Scale,
   and Anecdotal Record)
4. Student Test Record Form

Objectives and Test Blueprint

Discussion: The objectives below cover two units of instruction, as the test blueprint shows (Testing Periods 1 and 2). The objectives are stated in behavioral terms and include criteria for success. There are cognitive, affective, and psychomotor objectives. The test blueprint shows the relative weight given in the tests to each objective. It indicates the criteria for success on each test. The blueprint shows that the performance tests include checklist and rating scale measurements. (Chapter 2 discusses objectives and the test blueprint in depth.)

Written Test #1 and Answer Key

Discussion: This objective test covers objectives la, lb, and lc, as indicated by the test blueprint. The individual questions refer to the exact objective being tested. (These references are included for your information, and may be excluded on an actual test.) Note that question #5 does not completely test its objective (1b). That objective states that the student can select the correct blank. This question only asks the student to make a general selection, without seeing any keys. In other words, the student's theoretical understanding of the selection process is being tested. The performance test gives the student a chance to apply this general knowledge. If he is not able to perform the skill, his answer on the written test may give you a clue as to the nature of his misunderstanding. (Chapters 3 and 7 discuss matching test questions to the objectives.)

Examples of the three main types of objective questions

Test Blueprint

	Weight	Testing Period #1 Written	Testing Period #1 Performance	Testing Period #2 Written	Testing Period #2 Performance	Final Exam Performance
Introductory Locksmithing and Keymaking						
Objectives						
1. The student will be able to duplicate four major types of keys. This objective includes being able to:						
(a) Recognize and name the four types of keys with 100% accuracy	1	X				
(b) Select the correct blank for any key with 100% accuracy	2	X	X			X
(c) Recall the correct steps for duplicating keys by machine with 100% accuracy	1	X				
(d) Use the machinery to duplicate four types of keys with no more than two attempts per key	3		X		X	X
2. The student will demonstrate the honesty that is required of a locksmith						
(a) The student will state reasons for being honest (minimum of 2 reasons)	1			X		
(b) The student will recognize situations which challenge his honesty and defend his decision whether or not to make or duplicate a key	2				X	X
Criteria for passing:	100%		CL: 100% RS: 3	20 points	CL: 100% RS: 3	CL: 100% RS: 3, 3

(Student must pass each test before taking next test.)

CL = Checklist
RS = Rating Scale

are included: matching, true-false, and multiple-choice. The answers are easy to score because they are all on the right-hand column of the page. An easy to read answer key is prepared with instructions to the grader included in the "Note." (See Chapter 5 for information on designing objective tests.)

Introductory Locksmithing and Keymaking
Written Test #1

.... Score   Name ....
                                              Date..............................

Directions: You have half an hour to complete this test. Mark your answers in the appropriate blanks along the right side of the page.
   Match each type of key in Column I with its name in Column II. Use each name only once. (Objective 1a)

I	II	
1.	A. Barrel	1. ....
2.	B. Bit	2. ....
3.	C. Cylinder	3. ....
4.	D. Flat	4. ....
	E. Master	

Multiple-Choice:
When selecting the correct blank for duplicating
a key, which parts of the two keys should be·
identical? (Objective 1b)   5. ....
   1. The shape of the bows
   2. The grooves along the blade
   3. Length of the blades
   4. Width of the blades   a. 2, 4   c. 2, 3, 4, 5
   5. Height of the blades   b. 1, 3, 5   d. All of the above

True-False:
Answer true or false and correct the italicized word in the false statements. (Objective 1c)

The key blank is clamped securely in the vise *before* the carriage is raised.

6. ..T..F......................

The key blank is clamped into the *right hand* vise.

7. ..T..F......................

The sample key is clamped securely in the vise *before* the carriage is raised.

8. ..T..F......................

After raising the vise carriage, the sample key rests against the *flat side* of the V-shaped cutter.

9. ..T..F......................

The sample key is slid under the tip of the V-shaped *cutter*, while the machine grinds the blank.

10. ..T..F......................

Introductory Locksmithing and Keymaking
Written Test #1

Answer Key

1. C
2. D
3. B
4. A
5. C
6. F after
7. T
8. T
9. F shoulder
10. F guide

Note: 6, 9, 10 must include both parts of the answer to receive credit.

Performance Test #1

Discussion: This performance test covers Objectives 1b and 1d as indicated on the test map. The test includes the following parts:

1. Instructions to the student
2. Criteria for passing
3. Checklist of steps
4. Rating scale for assessing overall performance

The student's score on the checklist and overall rating are recorded on the Student Record Sheet.

This test measures the student's ability to apply the cognitive skills tested on the written test (e.g., Objective 1b, selecting the correct key). It also measures psychomotor ability. Only a performance test is appropriate in this situation, whereas the written test was appropriate for testing knowledge. Both tests are necessary, however, to give a complete picture of the student's skill level. (Chapter 8 provides information on designing these tools, and Chapter 7 gives suggestions on how to use them.)

Introductory Locksmithing and Keymaking
Performance Test #1
Student Record Sheet

Test Item	*Score*
1. Make duplicates of four original keys which will be given to you. Use the motor driven machines. You may have two tries to successfully duplicate each key. Passing = 100% accuracy (all steps on checklist performed correctly) *and* 3 or better on rating scale. (Objective 1d)	P N/P 1 2 3 4 5

Checklist for Making Duplicates
of Original Keys by Machine
(Objective 1d)

Check each step correctly performed:

... 1. Selects correct blank (Objective 1b)
... 2. Sets sample key in left hand vise
... 3. Clamps sample key securely
... 4. Clamps blank loosely in right hand vise
... 5. Lifts vise carriage to V-shaped guide and cutter (shoulder of sample rests against shoulder of V-shaped guide)
... 6. Adjusts blank so shoulder rests against flat side of V-shaped cutter
... 7. Clamps blank securely
... 8. Grinds blade of blank to same shape and exact dimensions, i.e., the new key works

Rating Scale for Making Duplicates
of Original Keys by Machine

Circle number on student score sheets which indicates the nature of the student's performance according to the criteria stated below.

1 = *Unacceptable Performance*, which is characterized by:
   —Taking more than two tries per key.
   —Any errors which can be attributed to haste, or poor visual judgment.
3 = *Minimum Accepted Performance*, which is characterized by:
   —Takes only two tries per key. (Note: On final exam, only two of the four keys can be attempted twice.)
   —Some slowness, awkwardness using the machine. May have to readjust the keys several times; or may work a little too quickly with respect to the level of his proficiency.
5 = *Superior Performance*, which is characterized by:
   —Able to duplicate at least one key on the first try. (Note: On final exam, all four would be duplicated on first try.)
   —Works deliberately; not too slowly nor too quickly with respect to his level of proficiency.
   —Recognizes the nature of any errors he makes and states correctly how to remedy them.
Criteria for Passing Performance Test
   100% accuracy on checklist *and* at least a 3 on the rating scale.

Written Test #2 and Answer Key

Discussion: This is an essay question designed to test an affective skill. The answer key shows a model answer and how the points should be allocated. It also includes "bonus points." Twenty points are necessary to pass the test, as indicated on the blueprint, but 30 points are possible. (See Chapter 4 for guidelines for designing essay tests.)

Introductory Locksmithing and Keymaking
Written Test #2

.... Score   Name ....
                                         Date ....

1. State at least two reasons why the locksmith should be an honest person. Your answer should not exceed 1/2 page. (Objective 2a)

Introductory Locksmithing and Keymaking
Written Test #2 (30 points possible)

Answer Key

An acceptable answer will include at least the following points:

 —The locksmith is the guardian of the internal security of the country, protecting both home and business. (10 points)
 —Honesty is essential to maintain the trust and confidence of the public. (10 points)

Additional credit will be given for the following points (in addition to the above):

 —Honesty is part of the ancient and honorable tradition of locksmithing. (5 points)

—Honesty makes the locksmith a credit to his trade; a shady deal makes him a traitor to those who have taught and encouraged him. (5 points)

Passing score = 20 points (10 of these points may come from the "Additional credit" answers)

Performance Test #2

Discussion: This test measures the student's application of knowledge of when to duplicate keys. There are three role-play situations which are scored by a rating scale.

The test consists of the instructions to the student, the instructions for the teacher, and the rating scale which describes level of performance. There is also an anecdotal record for recording observations. (Chapter 7 discusses methods of testing affective behavior. Chapter 8 covers the rating scale.)

Introductory Locksmithing and Keymaking
Performance Test #2
Instructions to the Student

You will be asked to role play two situations according to instructions which will be given to you. You are to assume the role of locksmith; your partner will assume the role of the client who is asking to have keys duplicated. (Objective 2b)

Introductory Locksmithing and Keymaking
Performance Test #2
Instructor Sheet

Two of the following three situations are used on the performance test; the third is used for the final exam.

1. A young boy asks to have a house key duplicated. He says his

mother sent him. Looking at the key you see immediately it is not a house key.
2. A woman asks to have two duplicates of a house key made for her children.
3. A man claiming to be a private investigator flashes an I.D. and asks to have a key duplicated. He acts as if he is in a hurry and does not give you a chance to look at his identification.

Observe the student and write down his responses on the Anecdotal Record. After the test is over, rate his performance according to the following criteria:

1 = *Unacceptable Performance,* which is characterized by:
   —Willingness to comply with any request, without further questioning of the client.
   —Appearance of gullibility or an indication of wavering in his decision in the face of argument.
3 = *Minimum Acceptable Performance,* which is characterized by:
   —Questions client further about his reasons for wanting a key.
   —Expresses reasons for the decisions he makes which are based on the evidence presented in each case.
5 = *Superior Performance,* which is characterized by Minimum. Acceptable Performance plus:
   —Astute observations about the clients, based on factors such as body language and general demeanor; uses these observations in reaching a decision.
   —Treats clients courteously and respectfully.

   Criteria for Passing = 3

Introductory Locksmithing and Keymaking
Performance Test #2
Anecdotal Record

.... Score   Name ....
                                                 Date ....

Situations Selected:
Observations:

Student Test Record

Discussion: This form is a sample of one way to keep class records for each of the tests taken by each student. It can be enlarged to provide enough space for brief comments about each test. For example, the teacher might note which objectives were missed, in addition to writing in the test score. (Chapter 9 provides suggestions for keeping useful class records.)

(Suggestions for administering these tests are found in Chapter 6.)

Introductory Locksmithing and Keymaking Student Test Record						
	Pat	Kim	Fran	Lou	Jo	Rusty
Written Test #1						
Perform. Test #1						
Written Test #2						
Perform. Test #2						
Final						
Grade						

Index